LAVINIA DOBLER

I DIDN'T KNOW THAT ABOUT WYOMING!

Books by Lavinia Dobler include:

A Business of Their Own
Animals at Work
Arrow Book of United Nations
Black Gold at Titusville
Customs and Holidays Around the World
First American History
Glass House at Jamestown
Great Rulers of the African Past
Holidays Around the World
I Didn't Know That!
It's Your World, Don't Pollute It
Land and People of Uruguay
National Holidays Around the World
Pioneers and Patriots
When Greatness Called
Wild Wind, Wild Water

**This book is dedicated
to every Wyomingite,
and to those who find
this state special.**

I DIDN'T KNOW THAT ABOUT WYOMING!

LAVINIA DOBLER

ILLUSTRATIONS BY WILLIAM J. LITTLE

Saddlebag Books
Basin, Wyoming

Library of Congress Cataloging in Publication Data:

Lavinia Dobler 1910 -
I Didn't Know That About Wyoming

Library of Congress Catalog Number: 84-062419
ISBN Number: 0-936457-08-2
Copyright © 1984 Lavinia Dobler

First Edition, Misty Mountain Press
Second Edition, revised 1987, Saddlebag Books

Printed in the United States of America at
Basin Republican Rustler Printing

TABLE OF CONTENTS

A black-footed ferret, a member of the weasel family, is one of the rarest animals in this country. A small colony of ferrets, found in the Meeteetse area of Park County, hunt for prairie dogs, their favorite food.

FIRST, RAREST
MOST SPECTACULAR

WHAT WYOMING ANIMAL IS THE RAREST OF ALL NORTH AMERICAN MAMMALS?

The only known black-footed ferret colony is located west of Meeteetse in Park County. This rare animal has a long, slender body, and can slide easily into its victim's burrow while hunting prairie dogs, its favorite food.

With a distinguishing wide black band across its eyes, this mammal, a member of the weasel family, looks like a masked bandit. Its fur is tan, but black hair covers its legs and feet as well as the tip of its tail.

In 1851, while James Audubon, American ornithologist, and John Bachman were working on drawings and text of their important book, **The Viviparous Quadrupeds of North America**, they studied the skin of a small animal found in a sparsely settled area, near the present site of Laramie, Wyoming. The scientists knew at once that the animal was of a previously unknown species. Audubon and Bachman were the first to describe the black-footed ferret.

WHERE IS ONE OF THE WORLD'S GREATEST FISH FOSSIL BEDS?

The fish beds can be found at Fossil Butte Monument, about ten miles west of Kemmerer, in the southwest corner of Wyoming. Millions of years ago, fresh water fish were covered with volcanic ash on the butte. Working in the Green River area in 1856, Dr. John Evans had found the first fish in the fossil formation. The 8,000-acre site was declared a national monument in 1972.

WHEN WAS THE FIRST MINING DISTRICT ORGANIZED?

The mining area near the Wind River Mountains, that would soon become South Pass City, was organized November 11, 1867. It's claimed that Jim Bridger, mountain man, storekeeper and guide, warned goldseekers of the dangers from hostile Indians. He reportedly said:

> "Fools and
> their scalps are
> soon parted."

Had Bridger been able to read, the mountain man might have been paraphrasing Alexander Pope's "Essay on Criticism," which contains the famous lines:

> "For fools rush in
> where angels
> fear to tread."

Many people rushed in to find gold in the South Pass area after a man from Georgia found some yellow rocks while trapping in a mountain stream near South Pass in 1842. He was later found scalped, with a bag of golden nuggets hanging around his neck. The event marked the first gold discovery in the South Pass region of wilderness Wyoming, seven years before the Forty-niners rushed to find the precious yellow metal in California.

WHERE WAS THE FIRST OIL WELL LOCATED IN WYOMING?

The first well was dug near the tar springs, a few miles south of Lander in Fremont County. In 1884, former miner Mike Murphy and his helpers, with picks and shovels, dug a hole in the red earth of the Chugwater formation near the Popo Agie River.

Twenty-five years before, in 1859, Colonel Edwin L. Drake had dug the first oil well in the nation near Titusville, Pennsylvania. The impressive celebration on Friday, June 29, 1984, at the Dallas Dome Field, the discovery site, marked the first successful oil well west of the Mississippi River as well as the 100th anniversary of the first oil well in Wyoming.

Union Oil of California continues to produce oil from the same field where Mike Murphy dug his first well. Although Dallas Dome Field was ten decades old in 1984, Murphy #1 and 70 other wells are still producing

Captain B.L.E. Bonneville, an American soldier born in France, in 1832 discovered the tar springs, located east of the Wind River Mountains, while he was traveling through this area. Indians had been aware for some time that the black springs existed. Emigrants who came west used the greasy liquid for medicinal purposes, lubrication for wagons, fuel and tack as well as liniment for their animals.

WHICH STATE HAD THE FIRST NATIONAL MONUMENT IN THE U.S.?

Located in northeast Wyoming, Devil's Tower is a 600 foot-high volcanic rock. The monolith resembles a giant-sized petrified stump, and is the most conspicuous and unusual geological feature of the Black Hills region.

President Theodore Roosevelt proclaimed the thousand-plus acre tower the country's first national monument on September 14, 1906. In 1933, the National Park Service took under its protection a prarie dog colony within Devil's Tower area to preserve for visitors a typical Old West scene.

The huge tower was featured in the movie, "Close Encounters of the Third Kind."

WHICH IS THE OLDEST AND LARGEST NATIONAL PARK IN THE COUNTRY?

Yellowstone National Park was carved from the northwest corner of Wyoming, along with the edges of southern Montana and eastern Idaho. The largest in the world, the park has more than two million acres of scenic beauty, mountains, lakes and waterfalls. There are thermal springs and geysers, some 2,000 of them, and over 260 species of animal and bird life.

President Ulysses S. Grant signed the bill on March 1, 1872, to create Yellowstone, the first national park in the United States " . . . as a pleasuring-ground for the benefit and enjoyment of the people."

WHICH MOUNTAINS ARE WYOMING'S MOST SPECTACULAR?

The Teton Range in northwest Wyoming and southeastern Idaho is the most spectacular mountain range. The massive granite barrier stretches from Yellowstone National Park to Teton Pass. Many claim that the gray-blue pyramids are among the most breathtaking sights in the American West.

Spectacular, with no foothills in front of them, the majestic Tetons, covered with snow during the winter months, rise high above sagebrush prairies as well as the winding Snake River and glacier-fed lakes of Jackson Hole. The highest peaks are in Grand Teton National Park. The most impressive and tallest of the peaks is Grand Teton, 13,766 feet in atltitude.

John Colter, a Virginian and member of the Lewis and Clark Expedition, was probably the first white man to see the awe-inspiring mountains. Traveling alone on snowshoes, he explored the area in 1807.

Wilson Price Hunt, enroute from St. Louis to the mouth of the Columbia River with his men in 1811, was impressed with the rugged peaks and christened them "Pilot Knobs." After they continued on to the Northwest, they crossed Teton Pass, which was originally named Hunt Pass.

When French trappers first saw the striking, pointed summits, they named Grand, Middle and South Teton peaks, **Les Trois Tetons**, that means "three pinnacles." Shoshone Indians called them **Teewinot**, meaning "many peaks." One of the tallest is still called Teewinot. The Teton Range includes part of the Targhee National Forest.

WHERE IS THE OLDEST STEEL BRIDGE WEST OF THE MISSOURI RIVER?

The old Army bridge over the North Platte River at Fort Laramie in the southeastern part of Wyoming is the earliest-built steel bridge west of the Missouri River. Constructed in 1875, the bridge was used extensively by the Army as well as stagecoach drivers on the Cheyenne-Deadwood Route. Those who were not employed by the government were charged a toll fee.

WHAT FAMILY STILL OWNS ONE OF THE FIRST DUDE RANCHES IN THIS COUNTRY?

For eight decades the Eaton family has owned the famous dude ranch or guest resort in Wolf, Wyoming. It may be one of the first guest ranches established in the world.

The Eaton brothers: Howard, Alden and Willis, who previously owned the Custer Trail Ranch near Medora, North Dakota, established their Wyoming ranch in 1904, at the mouth of Wolf Creek Canyon in the northern Big Horn Mountains, about fifteen miles northwest of Sheridan.

In the 1930s and 1940s, western resorts for dudes were profitable for Wyomingites whose ranches of 500 to 1,000 acres or more were located in the mountains of the Big Horns, the Wind Rivers, the Absarokas, the Black Hills, Medicine Bow and the Tetons. Some of them are no longer in the "paying guest" business, but are instead concentrating on raising stock.

WHO PREACHED THE FIRST PROTESTANT SERMON IN THE ROCKY MOUNTAINS?

The Reverend Samuel Parker preached the first Protestant sermon on August 23, 1835, a few miles north of the present town site of Bondurant in Sublette County.

WHICH TOWN WAS THE FIRST TO BE NAMED WYOMING'S "TREE CITY USA?"

Cheyenne was the first municipality in the state to be so honored, receiving Wyoming's "Tree City USA" award for 1982.

On April 30, 1984, District State Forester Dana Stone presented the National Arbor Day Foundation plaque and flag to Green River, the 1983 champion tree planting city.

Towns and cities in the state can apply for Wyoming's "Tree City USA" designation by fulfilling requirements set up by the National Arbor Day Foundation, whose headquarters are in Nebraska City, Nebraska. The program calls for the appointment of a city tree advisory board, setting guidelines for tree care and planting. At least $1 per person must be spent on trees within the city limits.

WHICH TOWN IN THE U.S. HAD THE FIRST J.C. PENNEY DEPARTMENT STORE?

Kemmerer, Wyoming was the site of the first store established by James Cash Penney in 1902, with two partners. Penney invested his entire savings of $500 and borrowed $1,500 more to open his Golden Rule Department Store in the small Lincoln County coal mining town.

Although there was competition from the company store where miners and their families usually shopped, Golden Rule cash-and-carry store prospered. Penney later expanded the business, setting up stores across the nation, and changed the name from The Golden Rule to J.C. Penney.

Penney's modest home, where he and his family lived for years, has been preserved by the Penney Foundation (as well as by the city of Kemmerer).

WHEN WAS THE FIRST NATIONAL FOREST ESTABLISHED?

In 1903, the Shoshone National Forest in the northwest section of Wyoming was established as the Yellowstone Forest Reserve. Theodore Roosevelt, one of the early conservationists, was president of the United States when the first national forest boundaries were created.

It was in this heavily forested area where Camp Monaco, "Buffalo Bill" Cody's famous encampment was located. Albert I, Prince of Monaco, with Count Beret, his aide de camp, participated in Cody's last big game hunt in September, 1913.

WHERE IS WYOMING'S
FIRST NATIONAL PARKWAY?

John D. Rockefeller, Jr. Memorial Parkway is located in the northwestern part of the state. To the north is Yellowstone National Park and to the south is the Grand Teton National Park. Authorized in 1972, it contains more than twenty-three thousand acres, and is bordered with lodgepole pines. The parkway is a tribute to Rockefeller's role in the creation of many national parks.

WHAT ARE WYOMING'S
OLDEST DOCUMENTS?

Petroglyphs and pictographs, found in many areas of the state, are the easliest known documents of Wyoming heritage where Indian artists created their symbolic arts on stone. Mary Helen Hendry, author of **Indian Rock Art in Wyoming**, published in 1983, has written that archeologists call the incised, pecked and abraded designs petroglyphs. Abraded means the designs have been rubbed off or worn away by friction or erosion. Pictographs are line drawings and painted designs.

One of the best sites to see some of the Indians' symbolic art is at Castle Gardens, some forty miles southeast of Riverton, or about eighteen miles south of Moneta in Fremont County. The site where the artists worked is well named for the brown and tan sandstone cliffs which resemble citadels of fortified medieval towns, landscaped with cedars, pines and wild gooseberry bushes.

Spiritual as well as ceremonial motives may have inspired the rock drawings, although there is still mystery surrounding the unusual artwork that includes the figures of hunters, warriors and many animals such as turtles, buffalo, elk, as well as birds. Some ten acres were set up to protect the rare petroglyphs by the U.S. Department of the Interior through the Bureau of Land Management.

WHERE WAS THE FIRST FOREST RANGER
STATION ESTABLISHED IN THE U.S.?

The Wapiti Ranger Station in the Shoshone National Forest is about thirty miles west of the town of Cody. It was established in 1903 when Theodore Roosevelt was president.

Wapiti (WAH-puh-tee) is the name of a large North American deer, commonly called an elk in this country. Wyoming has many elk herds, particularly in the northwestern part of the state.

WHICH RODEO IS CALLED THE "DADDY OF 'EM ALL"?

Held the last full week of every July, the Cheyenne Frontier Days' celebration focuses on the world-famous rodeo known as the "Daddy of 'em All."

Sanctioned by the Professional Rodeo Cowboys Association, a total of $430,000 in prize money in 1984, was awarded to 1,145 cowboys and cowgirls who entered many rodeo events that were featured daily.

The first rodeo was held in Cheyenne in 1896, the event being a one-day affair. Now the festivities run for ten days, with 100-unit parades featuring century-old carriages, Indian dances, chuckwagon races, concerts, carnival rides and an air show. Countless hours and talents are contributed by some two thousand volunteers each year to make the celebration a huge success, drawing large numbers of tourists from all parts of the world. Many observers, like the rodeo competitors, dress in Western clothing during Frontier Days.

HOW DID FATHER DESMET DESCRIBE THE FIRST WYOMING MASS IN THE WILDERNESS?

The Jesuit priest, born in Belgium, who had been attending the last mountain men's trade fair, left Green River (Siskeedee) Rendezvous on July 4, 1840, and traveled northward. His letter describing the service to a fellow priest in St. Louis was as follows:

"On Sunday, the 5th of July, I had the consolation of celebrating the holy sacrifice of mass ... The altar was placed on an elevation, and surrounded with boughs and garlands of flowers; I addressed the congregation in French and English, and spoke also by an interpreter to the Flatheads and Snake Indians. It was a spectacle truly moving for the heart of a missionary, to behold an assembly composed of so many different nations, who all assisted at our holy mysteries with great satisfaction ... This place has been called since that time, by the French Canadians, La Prairie de la Messe."

WHERE WAS WYOMING'S
FIRST COAL TOWN LOCATED?

Carbon, located fifteen miles southwest of Medicine Bow in Carbon County, was the first coal town. Two mines opened in 1868, the year the town was founded, which was also the year the Union Pacific Railroad first went through the coal mining town.

The peak year for coal mining was in 1888 when records say that 347,754 tons of black diamonds were mined. During the lifetime of Carbon, from 1868 to 1902, seven coal mines were in operation.

LARGEST, HIGHEST MOST FAMOUS

WHAT IS WYOMING'S HIGHEST PEAK?

Gannett Peak, located on the crest of the Continental Divide in the central Rockies, is 14,785 feet (4.202 m.) in elevation.

In 1842, Captain John C. Fremont, American explorer and soldier, with the famous mountain man, Kit Carson as his guide, climbed what Fremont thought was the highest peak in the Wind River Range. At the top, Fremont drove a ramrod into a crevice for the red, white and blue flag of the United States. At that time the flag had 26 stars in a field of blue.

Carson and Fremont then descended the ice fields, heading for the Green River Valley, but Fremont soon learned that Henry Gannett had climbed an even higher peak. Fremont, who is often called "The Pathfinder," had missed climbing the highest peak by less than ten miles.

Two glaciers, Dinwoody and Gannett, claimed to be 500 feet deep and eight miles square, spread in a fan-shape to fill the huge snow-covered amphitheater on the north shoulder of Gannett Peak. On the southside is the Bull Lake Ice Field.

WHICH WYOMING FORT IS ONE OF THE MOST FAMOUS IN THE WEST?

Fort Laramie, the first permanent trading post in wilderness Wyoming, celebrated its 150th birthday May 30, 1984. The fort trading post played an important role in the settling of the West and is considered one of the most famous posts in America.

William Sublette and Robert Campbell, two early mountain men, built a trading post and stockade fort in 1834 on the Laramie River, about a mile and a half above its junction with the North Platte River.

Over the years the old fort, originally named Fort William for the senior partner William Sublette, served fur traders, wagon trains and the Army. In 1841, the wooden stockade was replaced and given the name Fort John. The U.S. government purchsed the fort in 1849 for a military reservation, but it was abandoned in 1891. For fifty years it slowly deteriorated. Then in 1937, the state of Wyoming bought the fort and grounds, donating the historic site to the federal government.

High mountain peaks in Grand Teton National Park are among Wyoming's spectacular sights. Ranchers in the northwestern area of the state often build buck and rail fences (shown in the foreground).

During 1838 Myra Fairbanks Eells and Sarah Gilbert White Smith, enroute to Oregon Country to christianize the Indians with their missionary husbands, wrote in their journals, describing the fort on the Laramie River.

Mrs. Eells wrote:

> "...It is a large, hewed log building ... A fort in this country is a place built to accommodate the Company as they go and come from the Mts. to trade with the Indians for furs ..."

Mrs. Smith, on May 30, 1838, penned:

> "... There are no Indians here, they have all gone to fight with the Pawnees. We are among the Sioux. We see some females of white men. Last eve we received a call from one of the wives of some trader. Her attendant said that she had never seen a white woman & came three miles to see us. She was dressed in fine style. Perhaps her dress cost 100 dollars ... Her dress was mountain sheepskin, white & soft as kid."

WHERE IS THE WORLD'S LARGEST OPEN PIT URANIUM MINE?

There's a fascinating story concerning the discovery of uranium on a sandstone hill and the success of the Lucky Mc mine in the Gas Hills of Fremont County, some forty miles southeast of Riverton.

Early Sunday morning, September 13, 1953, Neil McNeice, who owned the Riverton Machine Company, and his wife, Maxine, a nurse, drove to Gas Hills by way of Moneta. Since it was open season, they would be hunting for antelope as well as prospecting for uranium.

When a few miles north of Gas Hills, Neil McNeice looked through his field glasses, studying the sagbrush and grassy countryside, and then at the hill some distance away from where he and his wife were standing. For some reason the mound of earth, sandstone and rock, later known as "discovery hill," seemed to have a different look.

Later, Neil and Maxine McNeice tested the earth on top of the hill with a geiger counter, the instrument they had used many times in hopes of detecting the presence and intensity of radiation. On that day the geiger counter went wild.

Excited, the McNeices collected samples of rock and sandstone from the hill before they drove back to their Riverton home by the Wind River. Neil McNeice immediately phoned

Lowell Morfeld, his partner and good friend. He told Morfeld, who had been unable to go out into the field that eventful Sunday, that he thought this time, at long last, they had found rocks on a certain hill that might contain uranium.

Since that historic day in 1953, millions of pounds of uranium U308 have been unearthed from the largest open pit in the world, and milled from the Lucky Mc claims. The granite monument at the top of "discovery hill" is not far from the mine, which was named for the McNeices.

Note: This material was taken from the article "The Uranium Story: Recollections of a Picnic in the Pit," printed in the September 1980 issue of **The Mining Claim**, authored by Roy Peck, **Riverton Ranger** co-publisher.

WHAT IS THE MOST FAMOUS GEYSER IN THE WORLD?

Old Faithful is in Yellowstone National Park, the largest and oldest national park in the world. The geyser, which has an appropriate name, erupts about every sixty-four minutes, shooting 11,000 gallons of hot mineral water some 150 feet high above the nearby forest. Nearby is Old Faithful Inn, claimed to be the largest log hostelry in the world.

The U.S. Congress founded Yellowstone National Park in 1872, from an eastern portion of Idaho, small section of southern Montana, and a large area of northwestern Wyoming. The park has 2,219,823 acres. The world's greatest geyser area has about 2,000 geysers and hot springs. There are also spectacular falls and impressive canyons that have been carved by the Yellowstone River.

WHAT WAS THE GLORY HOLE?

One of the largest open pit iron mines in the world, "The Glory Hole" began operations at Sunrise, Wyoming Territory, in 1887, and continued to operate until 1974.

WHAT IS THE LARGEST NATIONAL ELK REFUGE IN THE UNITED STATES?

About 7,500 elk spend the winter months in the National Elk Refuge where they are fed regularly. The refuge, which contains 24,300 acres of meadowland, including the foothills nearby, is located north of Jackson in Teton County. It's the largest national elk refuge in the country.

After the elk, in early spring, head for the mountainous regions farther north, Boy Scouts in the Jackson District, who have been granted a one-day permit, collect the large palmate antlers the elk have shed.

Later the Boy Scouts have the big job of bundling the antlers, then they weigh and tag them. An auction is held in Jackson by the Boy Scouts to raise money for the elk feeding program. The National Elk Refuge was established in 1912 by an act of Congress, and is supervised by the Department of the Interior, U.S. Field and Wildlife Service. Thousands of visitors go to the Jackson area to see the elk during the winter months.

WHERE'S THE LARGEST STEAM LOCOMOTIVE IN THE WORLD?

It's located at Holliday Park in Cheyenne. "Big Boy" was the largest steam locomotive ever built. Conceived by the mechanical department of the Union Pacific, Number 4004 was built in 1941 by the American Locomotive Company.

Altogether, twenty-four "Big Boys" worked over the rugged country between Cheyenne, Wyoming and Ogden, Utah. One of the Union Pacific engineers said about the giant steam locomotives:

"If one of those bulls won't go over the mountains,
it'll go through it!"

With the passing of the steam locomotive, Number 4004 retired in 1956. During 1963 it was donated to the city of Cheyenne by the Union Pacific Railroad and placed in Holliday Park.

The following are "Big Boy" specifications:

Total weight: 1,208,750 lbs.
Overall length: 132 ft. 9 in.
Coal capacity: 28 tons
Water capacity: 25,000 gallons
Driving wheel diameter: 68 inches
Firebox: 96 in. x 235 in.
Fuel: soft coal
Total evaporating surface: 5,889 sq. ft.
Maximum tractive power: 135,375 lbs.

WHERE IS ONE OF THE MOST FAMOUS MUSEUMS OF THE AMERICAN WEST?

In the town of Cody, founded by William F. Cody in 1897, is the outstanding Buffalo Bill Historical Center. The facility contains not only the Buffalo Bill Museum, but the Plains indians Museum, the Whitney Gallery of Western Art, Winchester Museum as well as Cody's boyhood home. The gray clapboard house was moved to the grounds from LeClaire, Iowa. Cody, one of the best known characters in the West, was born in LeClaire on February 26, 1846. He died in Denver on January 10, 1917, and was buried in Colorado.

WHAT WYOMING TOWN IS THE HOME OF THE WORLD'S LARGEST WINDMILL?

Medicine Bow in Carbon County in the southeastern part of the state has the world's largest windmill. It was built at a site five miles south of the town, and was dedicated in September, 1982.

Two giant wind turbines were constructed for the U.S. Department of the Interior's Bureau of Reclamation. They were erected to determine the feasibility of using modern wind turbines to generate electrical power. Together, the two turbines could have the capacity of generating 6.5 megawatts of electricity per year, enough for 3,000 homes. The tall wind turbines are expected to save 20,000 barrels of oil a year.

WHO IS CONSIDERED THE "ELDER" OF GRAND TETON MOUNTAIN CLIMBERS?

Paul Petzoldt, 76, founder of the National Leadership School in Lander, in July, 1984, completed his 60th anniversary ascent of the Grand Teton Range of Western Wyoming.

This internationally-known mountain climber was accompanied by a party of twenty-five, many of whom made the fiftieth anniversary ascent with Petzoldt in 1974. One member of the party claims that Petzoldt is now the undisputed elder of Grand Teton climbers.

"He's the oldest gentleman to climb the Grand Teton," Mike Zeno said, adding that climbs of the Grand Teton Range are well documented.

The book, **On Top of the World,** by Patricia McGarrity Petzoldt, formerly of Riverton, describes Paul Petzoldt's mountain climbing adventures in many parts of the world.

WHERE ARE COLLECTIONS OF INDIAN ARTIFACTS AND CULTURAL MATERIALS?

The Buffalo Bill Historical Center in Cody has the outstanding Plains Indians Museum. St. Michaels Mission at Ethete in Fremont County, has beaded and porcupine quill work. The Museum at Colter Bay has a rare display. The State Museum in Cheyenne has an Indian collection and many town and city museums also have artifacts.

WHAT IS THE LARGEST SINGLE REVENUE SOURCE FOR THE STATE OF WYOMING?

Oil makes up a large percent of Wyoming's assessed valuation. According to the State Department of Revenue and Taxation, crude oil production in Wyoming was valued at $3.2 billion in 1983, more than coal and natural gas valuations combined.

In the article, "Oil: State's Largest Revenue Producer," appearing in the **Riverton Ranger** on June 19, 1984, Publisher Robert A. Peck wrote:

> "Oil produced more than 50 percent of Wyoming's total mineral taxes in 1983, estimated at nearly $124 million dollars . . . Oil and gas property account for 57 percent of the state's total assessed valuation . . . Wyoming has the sixth largest proven oil and gas reserves in the nation."

WHAT IS THE LARGEST HIGH-ALTITUDE LAKE IN NORTH AMERICA?

Yellowstone Lake, with an altitude of 7,331 feet, is in Yellowstone National Park. This natural freshwater lake, with a total area of 139 square miles, is popular with fishermen from all over the United States.

WHERE'S THE WORLD'S LARGEST BAR MADE OF JADE?

The forty-foot jade bar is in the town of Medicine Bow at the Diplodocus Bar, and was cut from a huge boulder near Rock Springs. The tavern also displays trophy mounts from the Medicine Bow area.

Jade became the official stone of Wyoming during the 1940s, and has been found along the Sweetwater River and in the sagebrush prairies in Fremont and Sweetwater counties.

WHERE IS ONE OF THE WORLD'S LARGEST WILD LIFE SANCTUARIES?

More than 200 species of birds now inhabit Yellowstone National Park, including the yellow-headed blackbird. Bears, mountain sheep, elk, deer, bison, moose and hundreds of smaller animals live in the area that includes thousands of acres. One small mammal which intrigues tourists is the smokey-gray Townsend squirrel, often called a picket pin. It lives in the sagebrush and grassland.

Why are they called "picket pins"? Because they stand like sentries at the entrances to their burrows.

An abstract design of the first people in wilderness Wyoming.

FROM UNEXPLORED
WILDERNESS
TO JULY 25, 1868

WHICH INDIAN TRIBES ONCE HUNTED
IN WILDERNESS WYOMING?

Twelve tribes hunted in wilderness Wyoming. They were the Arapaho, Bannock, Blackfeet, Cheyenne, Crow, Flathead, Kiowa, Modoc, Nez Perce, Shoshone, Sioux and Ute.

IS THERE AN INDIAN RESERVATION
IN THE STATE OF WYOMING?

Yes, the Shoshone Reservation (now called the Wind River Reservation) was created by the federal government at the Fort Bridger Council in 1868. The first reservation to be established in wilderness Wyoming, it's still the only Indian reserve in the state.

Chief Washakie and seven Shoshone men, as well as Chief Targhee and several Bannock Indians, placed their X's on the document. Seven military men, representing the United States government, also signed.

The Bannock Indians left shortly for Fort Hall in wilderness Idaho, to be with their own people. The Bannocks never lived on the three-million acre Wind River Reservation.

WHERE CAN YOU SEE
IRON BEDSTEADS IN A CEMETERY?

At the Sacajawea Cemetery on the Wind River Reservation in Fremont County, a few miles from Fort Washakie, iron bedsteads can still be seen.

The Shoshone people believe that when a member of their tribe is buried, they should take all of their personal belongings with them. Bags, suitcases, Stetson hats, shawls, blankets and other personal belongings are piled on top of the casket, but beaded articles and deerskin clothing are placed inside with the body.

Long ago Shoshone Indians planted iron bedsteads on earthen mounds, using them as tombstones. A number of them, now painted white, are in the Sacajawea Cemetery at Fort Washakie in Fremont County, near the Wind River Mountains.

In early days Shoshone people placed the deceased's iron bedstead on top of the mound, using it as a tombstone. In the Sacajawea Cemetery there are many iron bedsteads, now painted white, on the graves of Shoshone men and women who died many years ago, but the custom of using bedsteads as tombstones was discontinued long ago.

WHO WERE THE FIRST WHITE MEN TO EXPLORE THE UNKNOWN WILDERNESS?

They were French Canadian explorers who were in search of the Western sea. In 1742, the year George Washington was ten years old, two brothers, Francois and Louis Joseph Verendrye, with two fellow Frenchmen, began an important, historic journey. After leaving the Mandan Indian villages in the Dakotas, they traveled westward, possibly as far as the high mountains now called the Big Horns near the present city of Sheridan, in 1743. But they abandoned their search for the Western Ocean because of hostility they encountered from the Shoshone Indians.

In the area where Pierre, the capitol of South Dakota, is now located, school children discovered in 1913, the lead plate that had been buried on the east bank of the Missouri River by the French Canadian explorers on their return trip.

WHO WERE THE FIRST WHITE MEN TO USE SOUTH PASS?

Robert Stuart, the American explorer who was born in Scotland, joined the John Jacob Astor venture on the West Coast, and in 1812, led a party of "Astorians" east. He and his rugged men were the first known to have used the South Pass and to have followed the main route that later became the famous Oregon Trail.

DID THE LEWIS AND CLARK EXPEDITION GO THROUGH THE WYOMING AREA?

Lewis and Clark did not travel as far south as Wyoming. During this most significant 4,000 mile transcontinental journey made between 1803 and 1806, Meriwether Lewis and his army friend William Clark served as leaders of the expedition. Among those who accompanied them were the dog, Shannon, a Negro man named York, Charbonneau, the guide, and his wife, Sacajawea.

The expedition reached the foothills of the Rocky Mountains in June, 1805, in what is now southwestern Montana. Later,

Sacajawea, a young Shoshone woman, served as an interpreter with those of her tribe. The Shoshones supplied horses for the men, and squaws to serve as baggage carriers over the Continental Divide at Lemhi Pass, Idaho.

WHO WAS THE FIRST WHITE SETTLER IN WYOMING?

Edward Rose, a member of the trapping party led by Ezekel Williams, who came into the area in 1807, was the first white settler in the Big Horn Basin. Ezekel Williams and the other trappers in his party are often referred to as the "lost trappers," because of reports of their wanderings.

WHAT IS A RENDEZVOUS?

A rendezvous is a pre-arranged meeting place, bringing people together at a specified time. The word **rendezvous** comes from the French verb rendez-vous, meaning "render yourselves" or "repair to a place."

From 1825 through 1840, American, English and French fur trappers, and tradesmen from the eastern states met with Indian hunters who traveled to attend the annual summer trade fairs in the Rocky Mountains. They were held in meadowland along the rivers so there would be wild grass to feed the horses and mules.

During the rendezvous, men sold or traded animal skins for much needed supplies and celebrated with friends and rivals.

Jesuit priest Father Pierre Jean DeSmet attended the last rendezvous in 1840, and recorded the celebration in **Life, Letters and Travels of Father DeSmet 1801-1872:**

"The rendezvous was one of the most interesting developments of fur trade in the Rocky Mountains... These meetings were great events and form one of the most picturesque features of early frontier life in the Far West."

Twelve of the sixteen summer trade fairs, called rendezvous, were held in the wilderness later known as Wyoming, in the valleys of the Green, Wind and Popo Agie rivers in sight of the Wind River Mountains.

WHICH EXPLORER BLAZED A TRAIL
FROM ST. LOUIS TO THE PACIFIC COAST?

Wilson Price Hunt and his party crossed the northern boundary into the area now known as Wyoming about August 1, 1811. Then, with his company of men known as the Astorians, Hunt traveled to the West, leaving by way of the canyon he had named for trapper-guide, John Hoback. They traveled through the somewhat narrow opening in the Teton Range now called Teton Pass.

Hunt's journey was important for it followed a route through wilderness never before taken by white men. In 340 days, Hunt and his men blazed the way across the continent from St. Louis to the Pacific Coast. By mapping out a central land route from the Missouri River to the Oregon wilderness, the vast expanse of prairie and mountains now known as Wyoming was thus brought into American history.

WHO NAMED INDEPENDENCE ROCK THE
"REGISTER OF THE DESERT?"

In 1840, Father Pierre Jean DeSmet, first Jesuit priest to travel through the Rocky Mountains, called the granite monolith the "Register of the Desert" because emigrants scratched their names on the hard stone. The unusual grayish-brown rock, almost 2,000 feet long and about 167 feet high, is on the north side of the Sweetwater River in present-day Natrona County. Many of the 50,000 names have been weathered by the rain and wind, but there are thousands that still remain readable.

The first meeting of the Masonic (A.F. & A.M.) Lodge, held in the area now called Wyoming, was at Independence Rock on July 4, 1862. A few miles south are Devil's Gate and Split Rock, both landmarks for the men, women and children heading westward.

WHEN DID THE AMERICAN FLAG FIRST FLY
OVER THE WIND RIVER MOUNTAINS?

John C. Fremont unfurled the American Flag on August 14, 1842. Thinking that he was on the highest peak in the Wind River Range, he climbed the mountain to implant the flag with twentys-six stars ˙ a field of blue, and the thirteen red and white stripes. Fremont was mistaken, however, for Gannett Peak is the highest peak with an altitude of 13,785 feet.

Orrin H. Bonney and Lorraine Bonney, in their well-researched book, **Guide to the Wyoming Mountains and the Wilderness Areas**, claim that Fremont climbed Mt. Woodrow

Wilson (13,500 feet plus). This peak is about one mile south of Gannett Peak on the Continental Divide in the southwest corner of the Dinwoody Glazier cirque. Climbing with Fremont were Charles Preuss, the artist, Basil Lejeuness, Clement Lambert, Johnie Janisse and deCoteau.

The next ascent was eighty-two years later, on September 2, 1924, when Dr. Carol Jones, the Reverend Albert Bessie and Dr. Edgar A. Doll climbed the peak via Route 1. The party named it Woodrow Wilson Peak because it appeared to have fourteen points. Following World War I, President Woodrow Wilson had proposed fourteen points as guidelines for the first major world organization, the League of Nations, which was dedicated to international cooperation and the prevention of war.

WHEN WAS THE FIRST FOURTH OF JULY CELEBRATION AT INDEPENDENCE ROCK?

The huge turtle-shaped monolith located on the north bank of the Sweetwater River was known as the "Register of the Desert" before 1847. On the nation's seventy-first birthday, weary-worn travelers who were bound for the West, assembled near the huge granite rock to celebrate the Fourth of July. Having no firecrackers, the men lighted sticks of dynamite. Many names were inscribed on the rock that Sunday, July 4, 1847. Since that time the famous monolith has been universally known as Independence Rock.

HOW LONG WAS THE OREGON TRAIL?

The Oregon Trail, used by emigrants for more than 2,000 miles beyond the frontier, extended from Independence, Missouri to the Columbia River.

The main trail followed the Platte River to Fort Laramie in Wyoming, passing through the Wind River Mountains of the Central Rockies by way of South Pass. It then ran along the Snake River and crossed the Blue Mountains into the Willamette Valley of Oregon.

More than 300,000 men, women and children traveled across wilderness Wyoming from 1840 until 1869.

WHO MADE THE LONGEST PONY EXPRESS RIDE ON RECORD?

Fifteen-year-old William F. Cody, born in Iowa, made the hectic ride in 1860. Called Will in his younger years, he was later known as "Buffalo Bill" Cody, due to his expertise in shooting buffalo that roamed the plains.

Will Cody mounted his horse, with the mail bags already securely strapped, and started from Red Butte on the Platte River to Three Crossings, seventy-six miles away. When he arrived he was told that his replacement rider had been killed. So without resting, he rode the eighty-five mile stretch to Rocky Ridge. He then made the return trip to Red Butte within the scheduled time.

The 322-mile trip is the longest on record for the Pony Express.

HOW MANY PONY EXPRESS STATIONS WERE IN THIS STATE?

According to Dr. T.A. Larson, author of the book, **History of Wyoming**, there were forty Pony Express stations, eight to twenty miles apart, along the southern part of Wyoming's wilderness.

The stations included:

Fort Laramie, Horse Shoe, Bed Tick, Deer Creek, Red Butte, Sweetwater, Split Rock, Three Crossings, Big Sandy and Fort Bridger.

WHEN DID THE PONY EXPRESS CROSS WILDERNESS WYOMING?

Although the Pony Express was in operation only eighteen months, it was an important form of communication before the advent of the telegraph. It began in 1860, when riders of the Pony Express crossed the mountains and plains on the emigrant trails in wilderness Wyoming.

HOW MANY BUFFALO WERE LIVING ON THE PLAINS IN 1850?

There were at least 30 million buffalo or bison on the plains in 1850. By 1882 only a few hundred were left. Ultimately, the herds were wiped out by climatic changes and the overgrazing of cattle.

IN WHAT YEAR WAS THE HIGH TIDE OF MIGRATION?

According to the first volume of **The Wyoming Blue Book**, the high tide of migration was reached in 1850. It is estimated that 60,000 emigrants and 90,000 animals followed the trails in one season.

WHEN WAS THE TELEGRAPH LINE
COMPLETED IN WYOMING?

In 1861, the federal government offered a subsidy of $40,-000 a year for ten years to the builder of the first telegraph line across the plains. Edward Creighton, the successful competitor, completed the Overland trans-continental telegraph line across wilderness Wyoming along the emigrant trail. The Indians called the telegraph lines the "talking wires."

WHERE WERE THE FIRST
TELEGRAPH STATIONS BUILT IN WYOMING?

Many of the telegraph stations were the same ones the Pony Express riders had used. They included:
Fort Laramie, Horse Shoe Creek, Deer Creek, Platte Bridge, Three Crossings, Rocky Ridge, Sweetwater Bridge, South Pass, Upper Crossing, Sand Creek and Fort Bridger.

HOW MANY EMIGRANTS TRAVELED ACROSS
WYOMING FROM 1840 to 1860?

There may have been as many as 300,000 men, women and children who traveled in covered wagons, on horseback, by mule or on foot, some even pushing hand carts across the prairie and over the hills and mountains.

WHAT ARE THE HISTORICAL
TRAILS AND ROADS IN WYOMING?

They were the Mormon Trail, California Trail, Oregon Trail, Sublette Cut Off, Overland State Route, Original Pony Express, Bozeman Trail, Lander Cut Off, Bridger Trail, Cheyenne-Deadwood, State Road, Black Hills Wagon Road, Wilson Price Hunt Trail, Robert Stuart Trail, Captain Bonneville Trail, Overland or Cherokee Trail and the Texas Trail.

WHEN WAS THE
BLOODY YEAR OF THE PLAINS?

The year was 1867. There had been trouble with the Indian tribes the preceding decade, but there were many more attacks between 1862 and 1868.

During the year of 1867, Indian warriors and braves constantly attacked the emigrant wagon trains and stage stations as well as the Platte Bridge site where, in July, 1865, Lieutenant Caspar Collins was killed during battle. The city of Casper in

Natrona County is named for the brave young officer.

General P.E. Connor came to this area in 1863 to protect the Overland Stage Route from Fort Kearney, Nebraska, to Salt Lake City, Utah.

During the 1860s, the U.S. government built a number of outposts, including Fort Sanders in 1866, a few miles from Fort Laramie; Fort Fetterman on the Platte River near Douglas, and Fort D.A. Russell, later renamed Fort Frances E. Warren, on Crow Creek.

WHAT IS THE
CROWHEART BUTTE STORY?

One of the most striking landmarks, east of the Wind River Range in Fremont County, is the large flat-top hill with sloping sides that rises high above sagebrush plains and alfalfa fields. Crowheart Butte can be seen for miles along highway 26-287 between Kinnear and the red rocks near Dubois.

Some years before the Shoshones were given their reservation in 1868, including Crowheart Butte, many battles were fought among a number of Indian tribes for control of the extensive hunting grounds in the Wind River Basin.

One spring day the Shoshones, under Chief Washakie, were hunting for big game in the upper country near present-day Kinnear, an area the Shoshones considered their own private domain. When they saw Crow Indians chasing herds of buffalo across their hunting grounds, Chief Washakie sent a young brave and his wife to the enemy camp to warn the Crow hunters to leave the Shoshones' Warm Valley at once.

The hostile enemies were furious and killed the young brave, but his wife escaped. Washakie then sent word to his allies, Chief Targhee and the Bannocks, who soon joined the Shoshone warriors. A long battle ensued because both tribes were evenly matched.

Legend says that on the last say, whether by chance or agreement, two angry chiefs, Washakie and Big Robber, met in personal combat on top of the high, flat mound. They raced toward each other on their war ponies, their spears, long shafts with sharply pointed heads, in position ready for action. When the powerful warriors met on impact, both chiefs fell from their horses. The fateful fight then continued on foot with Washakie the victor.

The winner cut out the Crow chief's heart and displayed it on his spear. Stories vary about whether Chief Washakie actually ate his enemy's heart.

One Wyoming historian wrote that when asked about the event, Washakie, then an old man, is reported to have said:

> "When a man is in battle and his blood runs hot, he sometimes does things he is sorry afterwards. I cannot remember everything that happened so long ago."

WAS FORT CASPAR A MAJOR OUTPOST?

Yes, Fort Caspar was a major fort in 1867, prior to the building of Fort Fetterman near Douglas on the North Platte River. About 450 to 500 soldiers were stationed at the military outpost during the summer of 1867.

The informative sign at the Fort Caspar Museum in the town of Casper reads:

> "Originally known to trappers and explorers (1830-1847) as Upper Crossing of the North Platte River, it became the Mormon Ferry in 1847. Guinard built a bridge here in 1858, and troops from the Platte River Station guarded the wooden bridge and protected emigrants on the Oregon Trail. July 26, 1865, the station was attacked by hordes of Indians. Lt. Caspar Collins led an heroic attempt to rescue Sgt. Custard's wagon train, but sacrificed his life in aiding a fallen soldier. The station was renamed Fort Caspar in his honor. Abandoned in 1867, the fort and bridge were burned by the Indians. The old fort was restored on its original foundations in 1936."

The museum is now located on the site of the old calvary fort.

Casper, one of Wyoming's largest cities, was named for the brave officer, but the city's name is spelled with an **e**, not an **a**. Lt. Caspar Collins spelled his given name with an **a**.

WHO INTRODUCED THE BILL TO CREATE THE TERRITORY OF WYOMING?

James M. Ashley, congressman from Ohio, on January 5, 1865, introduced a bill before the thirty-eighth Congress to create the Territory of Wyoming. It died, however, in committee. Ashley had suggested the name "Wyoming" for the Western land, and it alone survived the bill's defeat.

Three years later, on February 13, 1868, Richard Yates, an Illinois senator, introduced the bill before the forty-fourth Congress. This time it received the necessary number of votes.

The Wyoming Organic Act, which created the Territory of Wyoming out of parts of Dakota, Utah and Idaho, was approved July 25, 1868, by President Grover Cleveland.

(Source: **Wyoming Blue Book,** Volume I.)

Phatty Thompson earned a small fortune by selling Cheyenne cats in Deadwood City. But enroute to sell his cargo, his wagon upset, spilling cats in every direction.

FROM TERRITORIAL DAYS, TO STATEHOOD AND INTO THE 20TH CENTURY

HAVE CATS EVER PLAYED A ROLE IN WYOMING'S HISTORY?

Yes. One of the most unusual shipments ever hauled over the old stage route between Cheyenne and Deadwood City was in 1877. "Phatty" Thompson, an independent freighter who owned a wagon and mules, decided one day that the girls at dance halls in Deadwood City needed pets. So he offered twenty-five cents for every stray cat Cheyenne boys could find in alleys, around butcher shops and other stores.

After the teamster had loaded up the crate of howling cats at the Elephant Corral in Cheyenne, he headed north to the Dakotas. But Phatty met with disaster along the way. Enroute to Deadwood the wagon tipped over, upsetting the crate, with frightened felines running in every direction. The freighter did not give up, however. He succeeded in catching most of the hungry cats with food, probably enticing them with chunks of meat.

So once again he headed north. When he arrived in Deadwood City, Phatty Thompson was well rewarded. He sold the cats at exhorbitant prices, many for $10 per feline, and some of the girls paid as high as $25 for their new pets.

WHERE DID THE INFAMOUS CHINESE MASSACRE HAPPEN?

The Chinese massacre occurred in 1885 in Rock Springs. Only white men had worked in the Union Pacific coal mines in the Rock Springs area prior to 1875. Then when the miners went on strike, Chinese laborers were hired and brought to Rock Springs as strike-breakers. Less than two weeks after the white miners struck, the company officials fired them. However, work at the coal mines was resumed with fifty white miners and 150 Chinese miners.

On September 2, 1885, tragedy struck the mining town in southwestern Wyoming. White men killed twenty-eight Chinese; fifteen others were wounded and several hundred were chased out of town. Rioters destroyed property that was claimed to be valued at almost $150,000. Racial prejudice had been smoldering for quite some time and the white miners held resentment against the officials of the Union Pacific's coal department.

Acting promptly when he heard about the tragedy, Territorial Governor Francis E. Warren personally investigated the outburst and then sent a telegram to President Grover Cleveland requesting troops. A week after the massacre, soldiers escorted the Chinese people back to Rock Springs.

WHEN WAS THE LAST TREATY SIGNED BY THE TWO CHIEFS OF THE SHOSHONE AND NORTHERN ARAPAHO TRIBES?

Washakie, chief of the Shoshones, and Chief Sharp Nose of the Northern Arapaho Tribe, signed the last treaty on April 21, 1896, ceding the Big Horn Springs, north of the Owl Creek Mountains, back to the federal government. The two tribes sold ten square miles of the Indian reservation, land that had not embraced the mineral town of Thermopolis in Hot Springs County. The Indian people received $60,000 for their land.

The hot springs area is comparable to the famous Mammoth Hot Springs in Yellowstone National Park, and Chief Washakie was said to have wanted white people to have the springs for their health-healing benefits.

Arapaho and Shoshone people, especially the younger generation, enjoy the Washakie Hot Springs, located not far from Ethete and east of Fort Washakie on the Wind River Indian Reservation.

For years the people of Thermopolis have presented the outdoor play, "The Wedding of the Waters," with a cast of many Shoshone men, women and children participating, all wearing elaborate deerskin costumes that are decorated with the famous Shoshone rose and other beaded designs. The Indians from the Wind River Reservation set up their tall, white canvas tepees in the Hot Springs State Park for the event that is held annually the first weekend in August.

WHO SUGGESTED "THE EQUALITY STATE" FOR WYOMING'S NICKNAME?

Robert Morris made the suggestion. He was the son of Esther Hobart Morris of South Pass City, who in 1870, was appointed and served as the first woman justice of the peace in the United States.

A former territorial historian, Morris had suggested that "The Equality State" was an appropriate nickname for Wyoming, basing his idea on the action of the first territorial legislature, which in 1869, granted suffrage to Wyoming women.

The constitution of the State of Wyoming states in Article 1, "Declaration of Rights", contains in Section 2, "...all members of the human race are equal", also in section 2, "... political equality ...". Electors ratified the constitution November 5, 1889.

The great seal of Wyoming government is inscribed with the motto, "Equality State", and the word engraved on the University of Wyoming's corporate seal is "Equality".

WHEN WAS THE LAST
INDIAN BATTLE IN WYOMING?

The Lightning Creek Battle was fought in 1903 in Niobrara County, a short distance from the present town of Douglas. The last Indian fight in this state was caused by the misunderstanding between the Indian people and the white people regarding laws.

A Sioux chieftan from South Dakota, Eagle Feather, in October, 1903, led his twenty-five braves into Wyoming to hunt antelope. The Indian men resisted when Sheriff Billy Miller of Newcastle, with a posse of five men, tried to arrest Chief Eagle Feather and his band of hunters.

Both sides suffered casualties, but when the hearing was held in Douglas, no action was taken against the Indians.

WHAT DAM WAS WYOMING'S
FIRST FEDERAL PROJECT?

The Buffalo Bill Dam was Wyoming's first federal project, and has been designated as a National Historic Civil Engineering Landmark, the only one in the state that has received national recognition.

Lessons learned from engineering problems solved in construction of the Shoshone Dam, now known as the Buffalo Bill Dam, have been applied to other important reservoir projects in various parts of the United States.

The original name "Shoshone" was changed to the Buffalo Bill Dam by a Congressional act to honor the world-famous showman, Col. William F. Cody, better known as "Buffalo Bill". His home was in Cody, Wyoming, the town named after him.

Cody and Nate Salesbury had started the dam project in 1899, expecting the reservoir would mean the reclaiming of thousands of acres of arid land. But the two men ran out of funds and were ready to relinquish their water rights. However, the state later issued the rights to the federal government.

Begun in 1905, the 325-foot-high dam, built across the Shoshone River, was completed in 1910.

31

WHEN WAS THE BUCKING HORSE
PUT ON WYOMING LICENSE PLATES?

In 1936, the picture of the cowboy on the bucking bronco was drawn by Allen T. True of Denver. His brother, James B. True, was at the time Wyoming's state highway engineer.

Many people have claimed that the rider was "Stub" Farlow of Lander, and the horse was the famous "Steamboat". Lester C. Hunt, governor of Wyoming, and later a U.S. Senator, said he had Stub Farlow in mind when the plate was designed, but the cowboy from Fremont County was not really the model for the license plate, which is still considered one of the most distinctive and striking of all automobile plates.

WHAT IMPORTANT CASE WAS DECIDED
IN FAVOR OF THE SHOSHONE INDIANS?

The U.S. Congress passed the act (Statute 1349) on March 3, 1927, which enabled the Shoshones to sue in Court of Claims for that portion of the Indian reservation occupied by the Arapahos since 1878.

The Shoshones who sued the U.S. government, claimed that the Arapaho people had occupied their reserve, now called the Wind River Reservation, for sixty years without reimbursement to them.

Volume II of the **Wyoming Blue Book** says:

> "A final judgement of $6,364,377, less offsets, is reached (in 1938) in the Shoshone case against the government . . . After the cost of the suit and the government's non-treaty expenditures are deducted, the balance paid to the Shoshones is about four million dollars. The case clears title to the lands which the Arapahoes have occupied on a temporary basis since 1878, and the Arapahoes become co-owners of the Wind River Reservation."

WHAT ARE WYOMING'S EMBLEMS?

The state emblems are:
Flag: adopted in 1917
Flower: Indian Paintbrush, 1917
Seal: (The Great Seal), 1921
Bird: Meadowlark, 1927
Tree: Cottonwood, 1947
Motto: "Equal Rights", 1955
Song: "Wyoming", 1955
Gemstone: Jade, 1967

WHEN WAS THE TERRITORIAL
GOVERNMENT FORMALLY INAUGURATED?

The territorial government of Wyoming was formally inaugurated on April 15, 1869, when the territorial governor, John A. Campbell, took the oath of office. Campbell, who was born in Salem, Ohio, was appointed by President Ulysses S. Grant. Campbell had, in 1868, served as assistant secretary of war.

Cheyenne was designated as the territorial capital on May 25, 1869. That year the first census showed the population of Wyoming Territory as 8,014.

There were only four counties at that time, Albany, Carbon, Carter and Laramie, and it's interesting to note that each county extended from the northern to the southern borders of the territory.

WHICH BUFFALO JUMPS HAS THE
REGISTRY OF SITES ENROLLED?

At one time thousands of buffalo grazed on the plains in wilderness Wyoming. Indian tribes were dependent upon the bison for essentials, including hides and fur for their tepees as well as for wearing apparel; for the meat and fat for food and for cooking as well as powdered bones for the interior of the cradleboard.

White men also slaughtered the buffalo. In fact, William F. Cody, an expert marksmen, received his famous nickname, "Buffalo Bill", for having shot hundreds of these big, hoofed animals. Hunters often chased herds of buffalo off cliffs or into traps. In the early 1880s there were few buffalo left on the Wyoming plains.

Buffalo jumps and traps enrolled by the Wyoming Registry of Sites in the National Register of Historic Places include:

Casper Buffalo Kill Site, Natrona County
Big Goose Creek Jump, Sheridan County
Glenrock Buffalo Jump, Converse County
Vore Jump near Beulah, Crook County
Wardell Buffalo Trap, near Big Piney

The trap for antelope, which is enrolled in the Wyoming Register of Sites is Bridger Antelope Trap, Fort Bridger, Uinta County.

WHO WAS THE FIRST WYOMING INDIAN
CONVICTED BY A WHITE MAN'S COURT?

Yellow Eagle, a respected member of the Northern Arapaho Tribe, who raised horses in the eastern section of the Shoshone Reservation, was accused of horse stealing. A white man, Louis

One of the most popular events at Frontier Days is the bucking bronco contest. The celebration is held in Cheyenne every July.

Peterson, who ranched on the reservation, had accused the Arapaho of stealing three of his horses.

Yellow Eagle was arrested Thursday, July 12, 1887, and taken to jail in Lander. A few days later the trial was held in the Fremont County Courthouse, where the Arapaho man was found guilty and sentenced to prison.

There were many ranchers in the county who were indignant about the sentence. More than fifty prominent ranchers and county citizens signed a petition for Yellow Eagle's release, and Colonel Thomas M. Jones, Indian agent at Fort Washakie, interceded on the Arapaho man's behalf.

Thomas Moonlight, governor of Wyoming Territory, granted a pardon to Yellow Eagle two months later on September 13, 1887.

WHO WAS THE ONLY GOVERNOR OF WYOMING BORN IN A FOREIGN COUNTRY?

Thomas Moonlight was territorial governor of Wyoming from January 24, 1887, to April 9, 1889. President Grover Cleveland made the appointment. Moonlight, a Democrat, was born in Forfarshire, Scotland, and came to America at the age of thirteen.

His proclamation in 1889, made Arbor Day a legal holiday in the Territory of Wyoming, and reveals his Scottish-American philosophy:

> "It is said that a cerain man when dying, called his son and heir to his bedside and gave him his last request, 'Aye, be planting trees, they'll grow when your're asleep.' "

WHAT'S THE MOST POPULAR COMMUNITY SPORT IN WYOMING?

Rodeo. No holiday, such as the Fourth of July or Labor Day, or an anniversary of a town, could be celebrated in Wyoming without cowboys and bucking animals. Certainly the crowds would be disappointed if there wasn't a rodeo at every county fair.

Rodeo performers are not only young men and women. At the Old Timers' Rodeo, men, who in former years have won loving cups, belt buckles and cash awards, perform with enthusiasm as well as a certain amount of expertise. The audience in the grandstand hails them as heroes, even though the bucking horses and bulls often throw them.

Of course the "Daddy of 'em All" is the Frontier Days celebration that draws people from all over the U.S. and foreign countries. By far the most popular event is the cowboy, rigged in western gear, precariously seated astride a bucking bronco.

WHICH TOWNS CELEBRATED DIAMOND JUBILEES AND CENTENNIALS IN 1984?

Six towns had special birthdays in 1984. Buffalo, Lander and Saratoga celebrated their 100th anniversaries while Glenrock, Powell and Upton residents planned events for their towns' 75th anniversaries.

Activities ranged from parades and rodeos to costume and beard contests, craft fairs, museum exhibits, concerts and plays. One contribution to the Saratoga centennial was the publication of the book, **Tough Country**, by Gay D. Alcorn, detailing the history of the Saratoga and Encampment Valley from 1825-1895.

The author, co-chairman of the Saratoga centennial, searched for actual accounts of life on the Overland Trail. She went through over seven hundred different collections, searching for information. During the U.S. Bicentennial in 1976, Alcorn began gathering material for her first book, about ranching families in the Platte Valley. Sometime later she decided to write a book about her family and others who have lived in the area that is filled with historical events.

During Buffalo's centennial celebration in mid-July, the "Wild Bunch" held up the First National Bank and took the director hostage. The holdup was only in fun, and both tourists and Buffalo residents found the re-enactment exciting.

HOW MANY PREHISTORIC SITES HAVE BEEN DISCOVERED IN WYOMING?

According to a July 16, 1984, article in the **Casper Star-Tribune**, more than 35,000 sites, both historic and prehistoric, have been discovered in Wyoming, although ninety-seven percent of the state has yet to be surveyed.

The remains of extinct mammoths, camels, bison, horses and other mammals, have been found by professional archeologists as well as amateur enthusiasts, according to George Frison, former Wyoming State archeologist.

The Wyoming Historic Preservation Office exercises authority to protect sites only by federal law.

WHEN WAS THE STATE'S MOTTO, "EQUAL RIGHTS" ADOPTED?

The legislature adopted the state motto on February 15, 1955. Translated from the Latin, **Cedant Arma Togae**, the motto means "Let arms yield to the gown" or "Let military authority give way to civil power". In 1921, the motto "Equal Rights" first appeared on the great seal of the State of Wyoming, but it was not officially adopted until 1955.

WHAT PRESIDENT'S FATHER AND GRANDFATHER WERE WYOMINGITES?

Gerald Ford's father, Leslie L. King, and his paternal grandfather, C.H. King, one of the state's earliest entrepreneurs and wealthiest men during the early 1900s, lived for many years in Wyoming.

Ford's father and mother were staying in the elegant C.H. King home in Omaha in July, 1913, when their son was born. Several months later they were divorced. His mother, Dorothy King, and stepfather, Gerald Ford, Sr., were married in Grand Rapids, Michigan, and the young boy was then known as Gerald Ford to his schoolmates and friends. He changed his name legally to Gerald Ford, Jr., shortly after his twenty-first birthday.

Gerald Ford's paternal grandfather was one of the early pioneers in Wyoming. He first established a store in Douglas, and later, with his family, moved to Casper, where he was successful in transportation projects as well as the sheep industry. It is said that C.H. King was instrumental in getting the Chicago and North Western Railroad to extend its line from Shoshoni to Lander in Fremont County during 1906.

Leslie L. King was an officer in the lumber company in Riverton that was owned by his father, C.H. King, and by P.C. Nicolaysen of Casper.

WHAT IS WYOMING'S SLOGAN?

"Big Wyoming" is the slogan adopted for the mountain state which lies in the high western plateau of the Great Plains. With a total area of 97,914 square miles, Wyoming ranks ninth in size in the United States, and contains 10,028,300 acres of forested land within its borders.

During the 1940s the "Wonderful Wyoming" slogan was exclusively used, but a promotional campaign credited to Frank Norris in the 1960s was adopted as a more descriptive and appropriate slogan.

An extensive article entitled, "Tourism and the Economy", in

Volume III of the **Wyoming Blue Book** (published in 1974) is based on a report, "Travel and the Environment", that was written by Norris. The author presented his views at a "Discover America" organization regional meeting in Yellowstone Park, and during a lecture at an auditor's meeting in Cheyenne.

FOR HOW MANY YEARS
WAS WYOMING A TERRITORY?

Twenty-two years. Wyoming was admitted as the forty-fourth state on July 10, 1890, seven days after Idaho attained statehood.

WHISKEY GAP
& OTHER
HISTORIC NAMES

HOW DID WHISKEY GAP GET ITS NAME?

A northwest pass of the Green Mountains in present-day Carbon County made history when Major Jack O'Farrell, commander of "A" Company, Eleventh Ohio Calvary, gave the following order to his officer of the day:

> "All wagon trains containing whiskey are to be condemned and destroyed!"

His order may have been the first official prohibition enforcement action on record in the United States.

Drivers and passengers traveling on the Overland Route from Fort Laramie to South Pass had been attacked and harassed many times by hostile Indians. So as to avoid further trouble, a new route was developed south of the original one and went through the northern part of what is now Colorado.

The trail continued over the Laramie Plains, and westward to Green River. At that point the rough road would pick up the old route near present-day Granger.

Moving equipment, animals and the crew to the stage stations was a long, slow journey, and they were vulnerable to Indian attacks. The caravan desperately needed protection from hostile Indians, so a detachment of U.S. Army troops from the Eleventh Ohio Calvary accompanied the caravan from Devil's Gate Station to the West.

Emigrants also needed Army protection from hostile Indians, and joined the caravan along with a wagon train that was transporting whiskey, bound for illegal trade with the Indians.

At the end of the first day's journey, the troops camped some ten miles from Devil's Gate. Later in the evening, Major O'Farrell noticed that many of the soldiers appeared to be drunk. O'Farrell immediately ordered a search of all the wagons, and

After soldiers had drunk contraband liquor, Major O'Farrell, in 1862, gave orders to condemn and destroy all wagons containing whiskey. The spot is now known as Whiskey Gap.

the last one contained contraband whiskey. It was then that the commanding officer gave his order to destroy the fire water. The wagon train was fortunate Indians did not attack them that night, with so many inebriated soldiers "under the weather."

A full account of the event can be found in Phil Roberts' article, "The 'Good Water' at Whiskey Gap", in his 64-page booklet titled **More Buffalo Bones**, (Wyoming State Archives, Museums and Historical Department in Cheyenne).

WHAT DOES THE NAME WYOMING MEAN?

Two words from the language of Deleware Indians combine to make "Wyoming". Mary Lou Pence and Laura Homsher in their book, **Ghost Towns of Wyoming**, have written that the name is derived from a combination of two words: **mecheweami-ing**, which means "a land of mountains and valleys alternating."

Another source claims that the name was taken from Wyoming Valley in Pennsylvania, the site of an Indian massacre that became widely known by Campbell's poem, "Gertrude of Wyoming." But in the Algonquin language Wyoming means "large prairie place".

WHAT DOES POPO AGIE MEAN?

The name is of Crow origin. **Popo Agie** (pronounced puh-POH-zuh) means "beginning of waters". At the Sinks, about nine miles south of Lander, in the middle fork of the Popo Agie, the white-capped river, whose headwaters are in the Wind River Mountains, gurgles as it flows over boulders. Then it suddenly disappears, or "sinks" into a huge cave as it meanders through the unexplored underground channel. The Popo Agie rises again at a small lake about a mile north of the Sinks.

Large rainbow trout jump for bread that sightseers toss into the blue-green water. Tourists are fascinated by the gyrations the trout make as they compete with the other fish for tidbits of food.

DOES WYOMING HAVE
A TOWN CALLED CENTENNIAL?

There is a town in Wyoming that is known as Centennial. In fact, it's only village in the U.S. which claims that name. Centennial, located twenty-eight miles west of Laramie in Albany County, sits at the base of the Snowy Range in the Medicine Bow National Forest. In honor of the nation's centennial in 1876, the gold mine, discovered the previous year, was named the Centennial Mine. Later, the community that grew up nearby was also named Centennial.

FOR WHOM WERE
JENNY AND LEIGH LAKES NAMED?

The two Grand Teton Lakes in the national park were named to honor Richard "Beaver Dick" Leigh and his Shoshone wife, Jenny. Considered by many to be the last of the mountain men, Beaver Dick lived out his life in the Teton Valley of the Jackson Hole area in northwestern Wyoming, as well as the southeastern part of Idaho.

The Englishman became a friend to many famous men, serving as a guide in the 1870s for Dr. F.V. Hayden, head of the United States Geological Survey Expedition, which explored the Yellowstone region.

He also guided W.H. Jackson, the first man to photograph the Grand Tetons and the area that would become Yellowstone Park, as well as Nathaniel Lanford, the first superintendent of the national park. Theodore Roosevelt, the twenty-sixth president, was also guided by Beaver Dick Leigh.

WHY IS THE RIVER AT THE BASE OF
THE TETONS CALLED THE SNAKE?

The Shoshone Indians called the winding river in the northwestern part of Wyoming, **Yam-pah-pa**, after a plant they had found growing along its banks. The Indian women dried and then cooked the yam-pah-pa roots that formed a part of the Shoshone diet.

French trappers, who struggled with the rapids, called the river **La Maudite Riviere Enragee**. Translated into English it means "the accursed mad river".

No one seems to know whether the Snake River was renamed for its twisting, winding course, or for the Shoshone Indians who were called Snake People by neighboring tribes.

HOW DID BADWATER CREEK
GET ITS NAME?

For many years the Shoshones considered the cottonwood-lined banks along the winding stream to be among their favorite camping sites. But that changed one spring after a cloudburst caused floodwaters to roar down the valley near the foothills of the Owl Mountains, washing away the tepees of the Shoshone families camped by the creek. Many of the people were drowned before they could escape to higher ground. From that time on, the stream has been known as the Badwater Creek.

Today some of the largest flocks of sheep in Fremont County graze in the Badwater Creek area.

WHAT'S THE STORY BEHIND THE NAME RAWHIDE BUTTES?

The most graphic explanation for the name, Rawhide Buttes, which is located ten miles south of Lusk in Niobrara County, concerns a boastful young Missourian.

In 1849, while he was on his way with other goldseekers to California, he told the other members of the wagon train that he intended to kill the first Indian that he saw.

Soon afterward the wagon train camped in the east-central section of present Wyoming, where he saw his first Native American. The Indian was a woman, but the boastful young man aimed his rifle and shot her.

It was not long before the warriors of the woman's tribe surrounded the wagon train, and to escape being killed, the emigrants surrendered the killer to the Indians. Legend says that the Indians skinned the white man alive and then stretched his skin out on the blue-black buttes. Hence, the name Rawhide Buttes.

HOW DID THE TOWN OF TEN SLEEP GET ITS NAME?

"Ten Sleep" is derived from an expression by Indian people years ago. They measured time and distance in "sleeps" or overnight camps while traveling from one point to another. The site of Ten Sleep was ten day's travel from the Yellowstone area and the same distance from Fort Laramie - thus the name.

Ten Sleep is near No Wood Creek, named by settlers who were unable to find firewood along its banks.

HOW DID SIGNAL MOUNTAIN GET ITS NAME?

Signal Mountain, which looks out over the Teton Range, commemorates a man named Robert H. Hamilton, who lost his way while hunting in that forested area. The searchers agreed that if Hamilton were found, a signal fire would be lighted on the summit.

Hamilton's body was later found in the Snake River, and the signal fire on the mountain let people know that the man had been found.

WHAT WAS THE ORIGINAL NAME
OF THE SHOSHONE RIVER?

The Stinking River is the name given the odorous stream by John Colter after he left the Lewis and Clark Expedition in 1806, and traveled alone during the winter months to present-day northwestern Wyoming.

The resourceful adventurer was the first white man to explore the river. Colter called it the Stinking River because of the sulfur which permeated the area with an offensive odor. The name was not changed to Shoshone River until the early part of the Twentieth Century.

WHAT WAS FORT WASHAKIE'S
ORIGINAL NAME?

Camp Augur, at the present site of Lander in Fremont County, was established in 1868 as a military outpost to protect the Shoshone and Bannock tribes from hostile Indians. The name of Camp Augur was later changed to Camp Brown in honor of Captain Frederick Brown of the Eighteenth U.S Infantry, who was among eighty-one soldiers killed at the Fetterman Battle.

The fort was relocated in 1871 to the Shoshone Reservation in Fremont County and named for the highly respected Shoshone leader, Chief Washakie, in 1878.

Located some fifteen miles west and north of the original camp at Lander, the new site was near the confluence of the north and south forks of the Little Wind River. The Army post, which was abandoned in 1909, has since served as administrative headquarters for the Wind River Agency.

WHY THE NAME FREMONT CANYON?

John C. Fremont in 1842 was unable to float the canyon's white-capped rapids. At another rapids site in the canyon, the boat capsized, in the water, losing all records of his journey including his astronomical and barometric observations.

The high-cliffed canyon of many colors is now a part of the Alcova Recreation area and is supervised by the City of Casper in Natrona County. Pathfinder Reservoir, named for Fremont, a few miles to the west of Alcova, has been controlling the water that caused Fremont's boating disaster.

WHAT'S THE ORIGIN OF
THE NAME MEDICINE BOW?

The name originates from an expression used by Indian tribes who often camped and hunted in the southeastern part of the area now known as Wyoming. Indian people, who found birch along the banks of the rapidly flowing stream, made bows and arrows from the hard, close-grained wood. It's said that when Indians found a plant in the wilderness they could use, they called it "good medicine", so the river, too, was called Medicine Bow.

Because the glacier-fed stream's watershed originates from within the mountains, the huge masses are also called Medicine Bow, as is the town of the same name in Carbon County.

FOR WHOM WAS
THE LARAMIE RIVER NAMED?

The Laramie River was named for Jacques LaRamie, the French-Canadian fur trapper who was killed by Indians about 1820.

Fort Laramie lies within a wide bend of the Laramie River, which flows by on the east and south, thus forming Laramie Plains, then heads toward the Colorado Rockies.

Once a tempestuous waterway, it is almost dry in the late summer months, since much of the water is used to irrigate the productive Wheatland flats, once regarded as desert.

WHICH TOWN WAS MOVED
ACROSS THE BIG HORN RIVER?

Log and clapboard buildings in the town of Worland were hauled across snow-covered frozen Big Horn River during the early part of the twentieth century.

Settlers had anticipated that their town on the west side of the river would grow into a prosperous farming community. But in 1906, the Burlington Railroad started laying steel tracks on the east side of the Big Horn.

Undaunted, they started moving buildings to the east side along the track. Worland was then named in honor of a pioneer, W.H. Worland, who homesteaded in the area during the early 1900s.

The center of a farming and winter stock feeding area, Worland is also the seat of Washakie County. The town often celebrates "Washakie Day" to commemorate the building of the railroad.

HOW DID NEWCASTLE GET ITS NAME?

Often called the "Western Gateway to the Black Hills", the town of Newcastle, county seat of Weston, was named for the English coal port, Newcastle-Upon-Tyne. Many houses in the town, located in the northeastern part of the state, were once built on the sides of steep hills, high above the main street.

WHAT DOES MEETEETSE MEAN?

The Indian word means "place of rest or far away". The town of Meeteetse, some thirty miles south of Cody in Park County, is on the Greybull River. Meeteetse was one of the first settlements in the Big Horn area.

WHO CHANGED THE NAME OF THE SPANISH RIVER TO GREEN RIVER?

General William H. Ashley of St. Louis, Missouri, often called the "Father of the Fur Trappers' Rendezvous", changed the name of the river. In 1824, Ashley decided to rename the Spanish River in honor of one of his partners.

WHY WAS THE TOWN IN FREMONT COUNTY NAMED LANDER?

Frederick W. Lander was a young Army officer during the mid-1800s, and was placed in charge of surveying and building a new route for the Oregon-bound emigrants. The route, from Burnt Ranch on the Sweetwater River, some thirty miles south of the present site of Lander, to the Snake River in Idaho, was surveyed and built during the summer of 1852. It was known as the Lander Cut-off of the Oregon Trail.

In 1883, one of Lander's former scouts and guides, B.F. Lowe, established a townsite in Fremont County, along with E.A. Amoretti and P.P. Dickinson. It was located on the banks of the Popo Agie River. All three men had formerly been living in the gold camp at South Pass City.

Lowe then proposed that the new town and post office site be named for his former commander. The town of Lander celebrated its 100th anniversary in 1984.

One of the outstanding events was the eighty-ninth annual Pioneer Days "Pageant of the Old West" parade held on July Fourth. Ninety-two entries paraded down the main street, with historical and Indian-built floats of the Arapaho and Shoshone tribes as well as many fine horses, antique automobiles and sheep wagons.

WHICH TOWN IS ON THE NATIONAL REGISTER OF HISTORIC PLACES?

The town of Jay Em in Goshen County is listed in the National Register of Historic Places. Located about thirty miles north of Fort Laramie on Rawhide Creek, the entire town consists of nine structures and nineteen residents.

The town of "Jay Em" comes from the initials for James Moore, a cowboy who owned land near the present site of the village. Lake Harris, a homesteader, established Jay Em in 1905. His descendants still own the town.

WHY THE NAME BULL LAKE?

During below-zero weather, the wind whips the snow-covered ice on the glacier-fed lake in the Wind River Mountains. The cold wind lifts the frozen masses and drops them with a thud that sounds like the prolonged roar of an enraged buffalo.

One Shoshone Indian explained that the white buffalo's spirit is roaring with anger, and legend says that hunters chased the bull with the white mantle into the lake where it drowned.

Bull Lake, on the Wind River Reservation in Fremont County, is often called "The Lake That Roars".

HOW DID JACKSON HOLE GET ITS NAME?

David E. Jackson, a trapper working with General William Ashley of St. Louis, caught beaver in the rivers and streams in the area now known as Jackson Hole.

In 1826, he worked with William Sublette and Jedediah S. Smith. Jackson bought out Ashley's interest in the fur trade in the Wyoming wilderness. Later, in 1829, the men sold out to the Rocky Mountain Company.

The second word, "Hole", in the valley's name refers to the opening in the mountains which leads to the townsite.

FOR WHOM WAS TOGWOTEE PASS NAMED?

Togwotee Pass on the Continental Divide in the Wind River Range, was named for one of the last of the Sheep Eaters.

Togwotee (TOH-guh-tee) was not only a strong Indian leader; he was a feared medicine man and a dependable guide in many of the Indian battles. At one time he served as a subchief under the Shoshone leader, Chief Washakie.

The well-known pass, with an elevation of 9,658 feet, is within the Shoshone National Forest. Covered with lodgepole pines, the mountain pass is north of Dubois in Fremont County, and south of Moran Junction. Not far from Togwotee is an off-road lookout where tourists can have a breathtaking view of the Grand Tetons to the west.

FOR WHOM WAS LAKE DE SMET NAMED?

For the Belgian-born Jesuit priest who was ordained in the

United States in 1827. Father DeSmet traveled extensively in the western wilderness during the middle decades of the Nineteenth Century.

The Indians called Father Pierre DeSmet "Black Robe", after he had made a strenuous journey with his party over the mountainous country in present-day northern Wyoming. The priest and his followers arrived at the small lake, about six miles long, on Sunday, August 24, 1851.

His companions suggested that the body of water in the Big Horn Mountains be named in his honor. Lake DeSmet has since been found to be one of the deepest, natural lakes in the Rocky Mountains.

WHY THE NAME WIND RIVER CANYON?

The scenic high-walled gorge, known as the Wind River Canyon, has been appropriately named. The wind usually blows through the rather narrow chasm, helping to make more ripples in the fast flowing stream.

The river has two names: the Big Wind and the Big Horn. Countless years ago it cut through the Owl Creek Range and carved the deep canyon that is almost as varied in color as the coat belonging to David, the shepherd in the Old Testament.

Indian people called the glacier-fed stream the Wind River because the wind sometimes whistled and even howled. The headwaters are in the Wind River Range, north of the rustic, western town of Dubois in Fremont county.

Halfway through the Wind River Canyon, the river is known as the Big Horn, for the bighorn sheep, with creamy white rumps and massive coiled horns, which live on mountain slopes with sparse growths of trees.

Fossils, artifacts and rocks are in the magnificent canyon, with cedar trees and wild flowers, including the yucca plants that are everywhere. The rock formations range from the Precambrian period, the oldest and longest division of geologic time, to the Mesozoic period, the third era of geologic time.

The sixteen-mile paved road, with several tunnels, on U.S. Highway 20, follows the river through the Wind River Canyon that is south of Thermopolis. The well-known resort town with the world-famous hot springs and large buffalo herd, is located on the west bank of the Big Horn River in Hot Springs County.

"The Wedding of the Waters," one of the most dramatic pageants in Wyoming, tells of the Indian people who sold the hot springs to the white people. The annual event, held in the Hot

Springs State Park in Thermopolis, is observed the first weekend in August.

The Shoshone Indians from the Wind River Reservation set up their white tepees in the park by the mineral springs. They are the main performers in the pageant, and wear their beaded, deerskin costumes, which are often decorated with bright feathers and sequins.

The Big Wind-Big Horn River is one of the important sources of water to irrigate the thousands of acres in the once-dry sagebrush land. Big Wind-Big Horn eventually joins the Yellowstone River, then the Missouri and finally the Mississippi.

HOW DID SOUTH PASS CITY GET ITS NAME?

The prosperous gold mining camp in the late 1860s, located in the foothills at the southern end of the Wind River Range, was called South Pass City for a good reason. The present-day ghost town is some fifteen miles from the famous pass.

Thousands of men, women and children in covered wagons, on horseback and even on foot, traveled over the Continental Divide at South Pass.

Probably the most well-known resident to live with her family in South Pass City was Esther Hobart Morris, the first woman justice of the peace in the United States. She was commissioned on February 14, 1870.

At the east end of the main street is the reconstructed Morris cabin, considered by many as symbolizing the women's suffrage movement, not only in Wyoming, but in the nation.

WHAT ARE THE NAME ORIGINS FOR WYOMING'S TWENTY-THREE COUNTIES?

(Adapted from the **Wyoming Blue Book, Vol. III, edited by Virginia Cole Trenholm**)

Albany:
Charles Bradley, a member of the Dakota legislature, chose the name Albany, capital of New York, where he had formerly lived. The county was organized during January of 1869. Laramie is the county seat.

Big Horn:
Hundreds of brown and grayish-brown Big Horn Sheep, with massive coiled horns, at one time climbed the Big Horn Mountains, but they have been exterminated in much of the former range. The county was formed June 4, 1897, with Basin serving as its county seat.

Campbell:

This county was named for two men with the surname of Campbell. John A. Campbell was Wyoming's first territorial governor, from April 15, 1869, until March 1, 1875, when he resigned. Campbell had served as assistant secretary of war in President Grant's cabinet before becoming the territorial governor. The county was also named for Robert Campbell, who was a member of the William Ashley expedition which explored wilderness Wyoming during the 1820s and 1830s. The county of Campbell was formed May 23, 1911. Gillette is the county seat.

Carbon:

There are rich coal deposits in this county. The Union Pacific Railroad once had a mining camp at Carbon. After mine activity proved more prosperous in Hanna, Carbon became a ghost town. The county of Carbon was formed in January 1869, with Rawlins as its seat.

Converse:

Amasa R. Converse, Cheyenne banker and stockman, was honored when the county was named for him. He served as treasurer for Wyoming Territory from 1877 to 1879, and at one time, ran cattle under some twenty-eight brands. Douglas is the seat of this county, formed May 21, 1888.

Crook:

The county was named for General George Crook, who led the second Powder River expedition against the Indians. Crook County was formed January 2, 1885. Sundance is the county seat.

Fremont:

Capt. John Charles Fremont, often called "The Pathfinder", explored the wilderness during the mid-19th Century. He climbed one of the tallest peaks in the Wind River Range, and unfurled the American flag. He named the snow-covered summit, Fremont Peak, but it was renamed Woodrow Wilson Peak. Fremont County celebrated its centennial with year-long festivities in 1984. Formed May 6, 1884, Lander is the county seat.

Goshen:

There are two explanations for the name of this county. Goshen was probably derived from Gauche's Hole (Goshen Hole). The depression in the plateau in east-central Wyoming was named for the French trapper who set his traps for beaver in the area. The other explanation is that the county was named for the fertile land in Egypt in the biblical "Land of Goshen". Goshen was formed in January 6, 1913, with Torrington as the county seat.

Hot Springs:
Shoshones and Arapahoes sold a few acres of land on their reservation to the government in the now famous mineral hot springs in the City of Thermopolis. Hot Springs County was established January 6, 1923, with Thermopolis as its seat.

Johnson:
Originally called Pease, the county's name was changed to Johnson by the Legislative Assembly in 1879. A Cheyenne attorney, E.P. Johnson, served as territorial librarian from 1871 until 1873. Buffalo heads the county formed May 10, 1881.

Laramie:
The legendary French-Canadian Jacques LaRamie hunted the tributaries of the North Platte in the southeastern part of present-day Wyoming in about 1820. One early historian, C.C. Coutant, claims LaRamie was killed by Indians along the banks of the river that is now called the Laramie. His name has also been given to a military post, a river, a peak, a mountain range, a county, a city and a section of the Wyoming Plains. In January, 1867, Laramie County was the first to be organized. Cheyenne is the county seat.

Lincoln:
Named for Abraham Lincoln, the sixteenth president of the U.S., the county was formed January 6, 1913, with Kemmerer as its seat.

Natrona:
The county was named for the soda deposits (natron) that are found in that part of Central Wyoming. Casper is the county seat. Natrona County was formed April 12, 1890, by cutting Carbon County in half.

Niobrara:
Named for the Indian tribe that frequented the area, "Niobrara" comes from the Omaha Indian word which means flat or broad river. Formed January 8, 1913, Lusk is the county seat.

Park:
The county was named for Yellowstone, the first national park in the U.S. Park County was formed January 9, 1911, and is located east of the famous park. Cody is the county seat.

Platte:
The southeastern county is named for the river that winds its way through a number of Wyoming counties. Platte is a French word which means "shallow" or "dull". The county was formed January 6, 1913. Wheatland is the county seat.

Sheridan:
This northern Wyoming county was named in honor of General Philip Sheridan who served during the American Civil War. Formed May 11, 1888, the city of Sheridan is its county seat.

Sublette:
Fur trader William Sublette and members of the wagon train, started from St. Louis with 12 head of cattle and one milch cow, for the 1830 Wind River Rendezvous. The last of the twenty-three counties to be organized on January 2, 1923, Sublette's county seat is in Pinedale.

Sweetwater:
This county was named for the river whose headwaters are in the Wind River Mountains. The county was created December 27, 1867, by Dakota laws, as was the county called Carter. The county seat of Sweetwater is in Green River.

Teton:
French trappers described the peaks of the mountain range as **Trois Tetons**, which means "Three Pinnacles". The Tetons are considered one of the most spectacular ranges in the nation. Formed December 2, 1922, Jackson is the county seat.

Uinta:
The county is named for the Uinta Indians. The Uinta (Ute) mountain range is unique in that it runs east and west. The county was formed April 7, 1870, with Evanston as its seat.

Washakie:
Chief Washakie was the Shoshone Tribal leader for more than fifty years. The county, formed January 6, 1913, was named in his honor. Worland is the county seat.

Weston:
The county was named for Dr. Jefferson B. Weston, a geologist-engineer who was influential in the building of the Chicago, Burlington and Quincy Railroad in Wyoming. Weston was formed May 16, 1890. Newcastle is the county seat.

"WE WON'T COME IN WITHOUT OUR WOMEN"

WHO WERE THE FIRST WHITE WOMEN IN WILDERNESS WYOMING?

Narcissa Prentiss Whitman and Eliza Hart Spalding, recent brides of missionaries, not only were the first white women to travel in the wilderness now known as Wyoming, they were the first fair-haired ladies attending the mountain men's summer trade fair in the Wind River Range in 1836. They were also the first white American women to cross over the Continental Divide of the Rocky Mountains at South Pass.

These two women from the eastern states have the distinction of being the first white females to travel across the North American continent, having traveled from the Atlantic seaboard to the Pacific Ocean. Enroute to establish a Protestant mission in the Pacific Northwest, Dr. Marcus Whitman and his wife, Narcissa, the Reverend Henry H. Spalding and his wife, Eliza, and William H. Gray met the supply train on May 24, 1836, at Loup Fork, Missouri. The caravan was headed for the central Rockies, guided by an experienced mountain man, Thomas Fitzpatrick. There were the two women, 70 men and some 400 animals, mostly mules in the caravan.

Six weeks later, on Wednesday, July 6, 1836, the caravan arrived at the Green River (Siskeedee-Agie) Rendezvous. The extensive meadowland, where beaver trappers, Indian hunters and tradesmen often assembled for the summer trade fairs, was in the vicinity of Fort Bonneville, near the present site of Daniel in Sublette County on the west side of the Wind River Range.

Mountain men, who trapped beavers in the rivers and streams of the wilderness, were overjoyed to see the two gentlewomen. The Indian braves, their squaws and children were even more fascinated, since this was the first time they had ever seen ladies with white skin.

54

The missionaries conducted their Sunday services at the trade fair. Then on July 18, 1836, they traveled with the Hudson's Bay Company on the last lap of their journey.

That fall the missionaries, Whitmans and Spaldings, arrived in Washington where they founded a mission at Waiilatpu, now in the Whitman National Monument, near present-day Walla Walla.

A monument erected in Wyoming to honor the Whitmans and Spaldings is about fifteen miles from South Pass City at the historic pass, later to be known as the "Gateway to the West."

HOW MANY WHITE WOMEN ATTENDED THE 1838 WIND RIVER RENDEZVOUS?

Four American women, who were wives of protestant missionaries, arrived in time for the mountain men's trade fair rendezvous in the Wind River Range near the present-day town of Riverton.

A notice, written in charcoal and tacked on a storehouse door near Fort Bonneville on the Green River, told the following:

"Come to Poposua on Wind River and you will find plenty trade, whiskey and white women."

After reading the notice, beaver trappers, who had been uncertain where the 1838 rendezvous would be held, then headed their horses, mules and pack trains for the summer trade fair on the other side of the Wind River Range.

The four white women who attended the rendezvous on the Wind River with their missionary husbands were: Myra Fairbanks Eells, Mary Richardson Walker, Sarah Gilbert White Smith and Mrs. William H. Gray.

The missionaries had arrived on Saturday, June 23, 1838, with a supply wagon train from Westport, Missouri. There were 75 people and 150 horses and mules in the caravan. Also at the rendezvous were August Johann Sutter, who later built Fort Sutter in California where gold was discovered in 1849, and Sir William Drummond Stewart on his last visit to the Wind River Mountains before returning to his home in Scotland.

Journals written by the missionaries give valuable details about the rendezvous, one of the last ever held in the Rockies. Those who kept diaries included Cornelius Rogers, Mary Walker, Cushing Eells and his wife, Myra, Asa B. Smith and his wife Sarah. They also wrote long letters while traveling to the Oregon country to christianize the Indians.

Like Narcissa Whitman and Eliza Spalding, who were greeted with a noisy reception by the mountain men and Indian trappers at the 1836 rendezvous on the Green River, so were these women honored in a similar, somewhat crude, manner.

Myra Eells wrote the following, Thursday, July 5, 1838: " . . . Capt. Bridger's company comes in about 10 o'clock with drums and firing - an apology for a scalp dance. After they had given Capt. Drip's company a shout, 15 or 20 mountain men and Indians came to our tent with drumming, firing and dancing. If I might make a comparison, I should say that they looked like emissaries of the Devil, worshipping their master. They had the scalp of a Blackfoot Indian, which they carried for color, all rejoicing in the fate of the Blackfoot Indian, in consequence of the smallpox. . ."

WHERE WAS SACAJAWEA BURIED?

Disagreements among historians have never quite settled the question of Sacajawea's final resting place, or when she died. The young Shoshone woman has been called the "Bird Woman" by English-speaking people, but the translation has been challenged. There are also various spellings of her name.

As a young girl, Sacajawea was captured and sold to a Mandan Indian and eventually traded to Toussaint Charbonneau. As one of his wives, and the only woman on the Lewis and Clark Expedition (1804-1806), she proved an invaluable guide and interpreter when the explorers and their party reached the upper Missouri River and the mountains from which she had come. Carrying her baby son in a cradleboard on her back she endured the long rugged journey over the Rockies and west to the Pacific Ocean. The party then made its way back to a Mandan village in the Dakotas.

Some historians claim that Sacajawea, who was born in 1812, died at the age of twenty-five of "putrid fever" at Fort Manuel Lisa in North Dakota. Others, including Shoshone people, claim that Sacajawea died in 1884 on their reservation and was buried in an Indian mound near the Wind River Mountains.

The Wyoming Society of the Daughters of the American Revolution placed a granite monument at the Sacajawea Cemetery in 1943, south of Fort Washakie, on the Wind River Reservation.

Sacajawea is one of the best-known women in American history. Poets and writers have told her story and painters and sculptors have immortalized her on stone and canvas.

Mountain man Jim Bridger displayed the scalp of a Blackfoot Indian in an attempt to impress the wives of four missionaries, but his antics shocked them. They were the first white women in 1838 to travel across present-day Fremont County, Wyoming.

WHICH STATE WAS THE FIRST
TO GIVE WOMEN THE RIGHT TO VOTE?

When Wyoming was still a territory, male representatives who had been elected to attend the First Territorial Legislature in 1869 at Cheyenne, voted on a bill of world-wide importance.

The politicians adopted "An Act to Grant Women of Wyoming Territory the Right of Suffrage and to Hold Office," and Territorial Governor John A. Campbell signed the bill on December 10, 1869.

At that time, it's interesting to note, there was no suffrage organization in the sparsely populated territory. In fact the women had done no lobbying, nor had they demonstrated or presented petitions.

WHO IS THE
"FATHER" OF WOMEN'S SUFFRAGE?

William H. Bright, the Democrat from South Pass City, introduced the women's suffrage bill in the council, later called the Senate, at the First Territorial Legislature held in Cheyenne during the fall of 1869. Bright, a miner and saloon owner in the South Pass gold mining camp, was also first president of the 1869 Council.

When asked the reasons he introduced the women's suffrage bill, Bright explained that he knew it was a new and live issue, but he felt that it was just. He also said that he was determined to use all the influence he had to see that the bill was passed.

WHO GRUDGINGLY DRANK A TOAST
TO WOMEN'S SUFFRAGE?

At Wyoming's first territorial legislative session, members of the Council and House of Representatives collectively voted on the proposed women's suffrage act, and Governor John A. Campbell signed the bill into law on December 10, 1869.

Many of the legislators did not take too kindly to the suffrage law, but some who did not approve of giving women the privilege of voting and holding office, raised their glasses and drank to the toast:

"To the lovely ladies, once our superiors, now our equals."

WHO WAS THE FIRST WOMAN JUSTICE OF THE PEACE IN THE WORLD?

In 1870 Esther Morris of South Pass City was commissioned Justice of the Peace in the gold mining camp where she lived. She held office eight and one-half months and handled twenty-six cases.

Dr. T.A. Larson, the author of **History of Wyoming**, wrote " . . . the consensus at the time and in later years was that a Wyoming woman met the test of public office." Mrs. Morris had been commissioned by Edward M. Lee, Secretary of the Territory of Wyoming.

Among the interesting buildings in South Pass City is Esther Morris' home. She was chosen as Wyoming's outstanding deceased citizen, and her image stands in the Statutory Hall at the U.S. Capital in Washington, D.C., and also at Wyoming's capital entrance in Cheyenne.

WHO WAS THE WORLD'S FIRST WOMAN TO VOTE IN A GENERAL ELECTION?

The first woman to cast her vote in the Territory of Wyoming - in fact in the entire world - during a general election was Eliza A. Swain of Laramie, a gentle, 70-year-old white-haired home-maker, who was Quakerish in appearance.

Women were granted voter rights during the first territorial legislature in Wyoming on December 10, 1869. The following fall, general elections were held. The book, **Women of Wyoming**, (Cora M. Beach, editor), contains the following information about the historic event:

"On the eve of the election, Tuesday, September 6, 1870, she (Eliza Swain) put on a clean white apron, one of the belted kind tied in the back, with a shawl on her shoulders, a hat and with a little tin pail, went to the polls. She carried the pail for the purpose of getting yeast, possibly for what was called a 'starter' in the early days.

"Judge M.C. Brown of Laramie, a resident of that town and a practicing attorney, in those days before the famous 'first jury' and who has first-hand information of the events of that early day, is authority for the statement that she arrived at the polls early, and because she was elderly and so well and favorably known, they thought it would be a great honor to bestow on her, to allow her to be the first voter, and hence they opened the polls a little earlier than the hour set and allowed her to vote first . . ."

WHAT TERRITORY OR STATE HAD THE FIRST WOMEN JURORS?

The territory of Wyoming had the first women jurors. A few months after passage of the suffrage act in Wyoming, on December, 10, 1869, women served on grand and petit juries in Laramie, starting in the months of March and April, 1870.

Before women served on juries, the male jurors often interrupted their discussions of the court trial with drinking and gambling. But when women began serving on juries, those practices ended. In fact, smoking and chewing tobacco were also not allowed while men and women jurors were on duty.

However, in 1871, new judges on the bench stopped using women on juries. What reason did they use? They claimed that jury service for females was not an "adjunct of sufrage."

Seventy-eight years later, on February 19, 1949, the "Women Jury Law", (original House Bill No. 40), granted women the right to serve on a jury.

It's interesting to note that female jurors had a tendency to convict defendants and to recommend heavy sentences more often than their male counterparts.

WHO WERE THE FIRST WOMEN TO SERVE AS GRAND JURORS IN ANY COURT?

The women, all residents of Laramie, who served in 1870, were Eliza Steward, a school teacher; Mrs. Amelia Hatcher, a widow; Mrs. G.F. Hilton, wife of a physician; Mrs. Mary Mackel, wife of a merchant, and Mrs. Sarah A. Pease, wife of the deputy clerk of the court.

The grand jury met for three weeks, and among the cases the women and men jurors considered were cattle and horse stealing, illegal branding and murder.

WHO WAS THE FIRST WYOMING WOMAN TO GO INTO THE CATTLE BUSINESS?

She was Margaret Burke Heenam of Miner's Delight, a resident of the gold mining camp during the 1870s. Long abandoned, Miner's Delight is located near the ghost town of

Atlantic City in Fremont County.

Margaret Burke was three months old when her parents brought her from Dublin, Ireland, to the United States. Years later she worked as a seamstress in Cheyenne, where in 1867, she married Michael Heenan, a construction contractor for the Union Pacific Railroad. Excited by the gold rush in the South Pass City - Atlantic City region, they moved to Miner's Delight near the Wind River Mountains.

Then tragedy struck, leaving Margaret a widow when her husband, while working as a teamster, was ambushed and brutally scalped by Indians at Twin Creek Hill on September 17, 1872, as he was bringing in a wagonload of hay from the Lander Valley.

Not long after their daughter was born prematurely, the widowed mother of three opened up a boarding house in her cabin near Spring Gulch. Her boarders were prospectors, freighters and transient travelers. The miners paid Mrs. Heenan for their meals with gold nuggets that she placed in a large pickle jar. When the jar in her kitchen was full, she traded the nuggets for some cattle.

It wasn't long before she had a fair-sized herd grazing in the meadowland along Spring Gulch near the mining camp. Her cattle were branded with a "Circle H" in memory of her late husband.

On August 16, 1875, she married Peter P. Dickinson, who was later one of the founding fathers of the town of Lander, established in 1884. The Dickinsons lived on Main Street where they managed the Dickinson Hotel. The couple also ran cattle in the Wind River Mountains in an area now called Dickinson Park.

Mrs. Dickinson organized the first public school in Lander. She secured a land grant for both the Episcopal and Catholic churches in Lander, as well as getting land for the Episcopal Church in Shoshoni. She also organized the first Sunday School to be held in Lander.

Mrs. Dickinson was the first woman to serve on the Lander School Board, and was often a delegate to the Wyoming State Democratic Conventions. On two occasions she was the alternate to the National Democratic Conventions.

She gave each of her grandchildren a calf to raise, and although the three Dobler girls of Riverton (Virginia, Lavinia and Frances) weren't related by blood, she gave them a calf which was raised in a small barn in the backyard by the alley at Monroe Avenue and Third Street. Their aunt, Gertrude Dobler, a teacher in Lander, married William, the Dickinson's only son.

WHO SAID OR WROTE
"WE WON'T COME IN WITHOUT OUR WOMEN?"

Extensive research has not revealed the occasion for the above quotation. There were many serious problems to face in 1890, when Wyoming congressmen requested that statehood be granted the sparsely populated territory.

Perhaps, when it was learned that the suffrage law had been enacted, there would be even more problems with politicians from other states, who were not in favor of such legislation. But determined Wyomingites may have telegraphed or written to their own congressmen in Washington, D.C., stating: "We won't come in without our women."

WHO WAS THE FIRST WOMAN
TO BE ELECTED TO A STATE OFFICE?

Estelle Reel, born in Pittsfield, Illinois, was thirty-six years old in 1894, when she was elected to the post of superintendent of public instruction in Wyoming. A Republican, she had the honor of being the first woman in the country elected to a state office. Another interesting fact is that Estelle Reel received the largest number of votes ever given a candidate in the state of Wyoming at that time.

She took over the duties as head of the state education office on January 7, 1895, serving until January 27, 1898. She resigned to accept another responsible position when President William McKinley appointed her National Superintendent of Indian Schools, and she was unanimously confirmed in 1898 by the United States Senate. Twelve years later, in 1910, she married Cort F. Meyer of Washington.

WHO WAS THE FIRST WOMAN ELECTED
TO A STATE LEGISLATURE IN THE U.S.?

Mary G. Bellamy of Laramie represented Albany County in 1911. She was the first woman elected to a state legislature in this country. Then two women, Anna B. Miller of Albany county and Nettie Truax of Crook and Campbell counties, served in the 1913 legislature. Since that time, many women have served.

Mary Bellamy went to Washington in 1917, to represent Wyoming women during the national campaign for the Nineteenth Amendment, the National Suffrage Bill.

WHO MAY HAVE BEEN THE FIRST WOMAN MAYOR IN THE UNITED STATES?

In 1911, the small western town of Dayton, located northwest of Sheridan, attracted considerable attention by electing Susan Wissler its mayor. Dayton residents, at that time, claimed that Mrs. Wissler was the first woman mayor in this country, but the honor has since been disputed.

WHO DRAFTED THE BILL FOR THE STATE FLOWER?

Dr. Grace Raymond Hebard of the University of Wyoming drafted the bill. She also personally employed the New York artist, Margaret Armstrong, to paint a picture of the Indian paintbrush. The bill had been recommended for passage by the Laramie Chapter of the Daughters of the American Revolution. (**Wyoming Blue Book**, Vol. II).

The Indian paintbrush became the state flower on Tuesday, January 31, 1917, the same day the Fourteenth Legislature adopted the Wyoming state flag, designed by Vera Keays of Buffalo.

George F. Dobler, lawyer from Riverton, and the father of this author, at that session was serving as chairman of the Judiciary Committee in the House of Representatives. He voted for the state flower, the Wyoming paintbrush.

In the reference book, **A Field Guide to Rocky Mountain Wildflowers**, written by John J. Craighead, Frank C. Craighead, Jr., and Ray J. Davis, the scientists list the flower's botanical name, **Castilleja linariaefolia**, as the Wyoming paintbrush. Other names for the flower are painted-cup and Wyoming painted cup.

When in June, July and the first part of August, in full bloom, the highly colored bracts and upper leaves as well as the red or scarlet leaflike bracts below each yellowish-green flower make a brillant impression on the landscape.

WHO WAS THE FIRST WYOMING WOMAN FOUND GUILTY IN COURT OF RUSTLING?

Anna Richey was found guilty of cattle rustling during November of 1919, in the area of Kemmerer. Although some of the ranchers described her as "thirty, purty and full of life," a Lincoln County judge sentenced her to prison.

She was known in southwestern Wyoming as "Queen Anna" because she sat well in the saddle, handling her horse with dignity and grace. A woman of culture, Anna Richey was the daughter of a wealthy rancher. She'd had many suitors before she married a teacher, from whom she was later divorced.

Some of the ranchers considered Anna too ambitious for a woman, and some were aware that she was impatient to enlarge her herd of cattle. In July, 1919, Anna Richey rounded up thirty-two head of cattle that did not belong to her. At Fossil, not far from the now-famous Fossil Butte, she loaded them onto railroad cars and had them shipped to Omaha, Nebraska.

So Anna was accused of rustling. On the way to the trial, she was shot by a masked rider and was hospitalized. She recovered in time to be found guilty of rustling and altering eight brands. Sentenced to six years in the state penitentiary, she was free on bond to wind up her ranch business, but died suddenly while working with her hired man.

Rumors said she had been poisoned and ranchers in the Ham's Fork area claimed that she had been talking to a stranger the day before she died. But the reason for her death still remains a mystery.

WHO DESIGNED THE STATE FLAG?

Verna Keays of Buffalo designed the state flag. Thirty-seven designs were submitted in the contest conducted by the Daughters of the American Revolution. In March of 1919 the flag's designer (later Mrs. A.C. Keyes), donated the original sketch of the state flag to the Wyoming Historical Department.

Mrs. Keyes wrote the following legend of the Wyoming state flag:

> "The Great Seal of the State of Wyoming is the heart of the flag.
>
> The seal of the bison represents the truly western custom of branding. The bison was once 'monarch of the plains.'
>
> The red border represents the red man, who knew and loved our country long before any of us were here; also, the blood of the pioneers who gave their lives reclaiming the soil.
>
> White is an emblem of purity and uprightness over Wyoming.
>
> Blue, which is found in the bluest of blue Wyoming skies and the distant mountains, has through the ages been significant of fidelity, justice and virility.
>
> And finally, the red, the white, and the blue of the flag of the state of Wyoming are the colors of the

greatest flag in all the world, the stars and stripes of the United States of America."

The Wyoming state flag was adopted by the legislature, January 31, 1917. The Indian paintbrush became the state flower at the same time.

WHO WAS THE FIRST WOMAN GOVERNOR IN THE UNITED STATES?

Nellie Taloe Ross of Wyoming, who was elected to fill the last two years of her husband's unexpired term , became the governor of Wyoming on Monday, January 5, 1925. A few days later, Miriam Wallace Ferguson, also elected in 1924, became the first woman governor of Texas, and like Mrs. Ross, was a Democrat who served from 1925-1927.

Mrs. Ross also held the distinction of being the first woman director of the U.S. Mint in Washington, D.C. The appointment was made in April, 1933.

Two of Wyoming's "first ladies", Thyra Thomson, the first woman secretary of state, and Nellie Taloe Ross, then 92 years old, attended the Yellowstone Park Centennial in 1972.

DO WOMEN SERVE ON TRIBAL COUNCILS ON THE WIND RIVER RESERVATION?

Yes, the Arapaho and Shoshone tribes permitted women to serve on the two tribal councils before the Wyoming Supreme Court unanimously upheld the constitutionality of the "Women on Jury Act" passed by the state legislature in 1949. **(Wyoming Blue Book).**

WHO WAS THE FIRST WOMAN ELECTED TO THE SHOSHONE TRIBAL COUNCIL?

In 1930, Irene Kinnear Mead, granddaughter of Jim Baker, famous American trapper and mountain man originally from Illinois, was the first Shoshone woman elected to the Tribal Council. At the meetings held on the Wind River Reservation, council members decide on matters pertaining to the several thousand Shoshone men, women and children, most of whom live in comfortable wooden homes, not tepees, in sight of the Wind River Mountains.

The Shoshones and Arapahos receive annual royalty payments for oil produced on their reservation. Most Indian families drive pickup trucks and passenger cars to get supplies in the neighboring towns, Riverton and Lander in Fremont County, in sharp contrast to the wagons drawn by horses the Indian people used for transportation not too many decades ago.

The Wyoming town of Kinnear, was named for Irene Kinnear Mead's father, Napoleon Bonaparte Kinnear, who lived on a Fremont County ranch.

WHEN DID NELLIE SCOTT BEGIN HER TERM ON THE ARAPAHO TRIBAL COUNCIL?

Nellie Scott, whose mother as a child was found abandoned on a battlefield by Indian warriors, in 1937 began her first term on the Arapaho Tribal Council. Mrs. Scott was the second woman to be elected to one of the two tribal councils on the Wind River Reservation. Irene Kinnear Mead, a member of the Shoshone Tribe, was the first.

Nellie Scott has the distinction of having been listed on both council rolls, but because of a technicality, she was dropped by the Shoshones although she was later placed on the Arapaho tribal roll by Chief Yellow Calf.

Mrs. Scott was 83 years old in 1974, when she had served more than thirty years on the Arapaho Tribal Council. Her white bungalow, surrounded by a well-kept lawn and perennial flowers, was not far from the Indian agency at Fort Washakie.

TO WHOM WERE THE FIRST BOOKS GIVEN FOR THE "WYOMING LIBRARY"?

In 1967, a special "Wyoming Library" was started at a regional meeting of the Rocky Mountain Press Women, held in Laramie.

Sixty-four books, non-fiction as well as story and poetry collections by Wyoming authors, or on subjects pertaining to the state, were presented to Roberta "Bobby" Hathaway, first lady of Wyoming, and wife of Governor Stan K. Hathaway.

With the aid of the Wyoming Press Women, the "Wyoming Library" was set up in the governor's mansion in Cheyenne. In 1984, the collection had grown in value and interest since 1967. There are now 225 books in the living room of the governor's mansion. The books are not available to the public, but guests at the mansion are impressed with the wealth of material about the state in the Wyoming collection.

WAS A CASPER WRITER WYOMING'S FIRST POET LAUREATE?

Peggy Simson Curry of Casper was honored as Wyoming's first poet laureate in January, 1981, by Ed Herschler, governor of Wyoming. Her book length narrative poem, **Red Wind of Wyoming**, about the Johnson County War in 1892 near Buffalo, was adapted as a radio drama in 1969 by Frank Parman. The author, who had been reading Asa Mercer's **Banditti of the Plains**, conceived the idea for her poem while sitting in Casper's old Elbow Room Lounge in the Henning Hotel.

Johnson County was invaded by "regulars", stockmen and Texas gunmen who tried to put a stop to cattle rustling with armed force. The Johnson County War continues to be one of the most controversial and publicized events in the state's history.

Wyoming Writers honored Peggy Simson Curry with two "Emmie Mygatt" awards for her outstanding service to writers within the state. Western Writers of America presented her with two "Spur Awards" in the fields of juvenile and adult fiction.

She considered **So Far From Spring** her best novel. This Western novel as well as **The Oil Patch** and **Fire in the Water** have all been translated into at least eight languages.

The Casper resident served as chairman of the Wyoming Bicentennial Commission in 1976, and her life story is described in Jean Mead's book, **Wyoming in Profile**. Peggy Curry had lived in Wyoming for more than forty years. She died in 1986.

WHO WAS GIVEN THE TITLE "GRAND LADY OF THE BOZEMAN TRAIL?"

Elsa Spear Byron, born near Big Horn, and one of the descendants of one of Wyoming's first families, was given the title, "Grand Lady of the Bozeman Trail" by National Geographic in its 1979 edition of the book, **Trails West**. She was named as one of three outstanding artist-photographers by the University of Wyoming in 1976. Elsa Spear Byron was also the recipient of the Trustees Award in 1982 from the National Cowboy Hall of Fame in Oklahoma City.

Author of three books on Wyoming history, she is the Big Horn area's authority on the Bozeman Trail, Fort Phil Kearney and other regional history.

She was honored by Governor Ed Herschler on June 2, 1984, when he proclaimed "Elsa Spear Byron Day", and by Wyoming Writers at their workshop in Sheridan on the same day. Gene M. Gressley, archivist and head of the Western History Research Center of the University of Wyoming, also spoke of her contributions to the state.

Her father, Willis M. Spear, and three other family members, moved to the Big Horn area from Montana in 1883, bringing along 100 head of cattle and 175 horses. In 1923, the Spear family opened Spear-O-Wigwam in the Big Horn Mountains to cater to the dude trade.

Interest in Elsa's photography soared that year when she led a group of women from a September mountain blizzard, blacking their faces with charcoal, tearing up gunny sacks for their feet, while snapping photographs along the way. By Christmas, seventy of the pictures had been sold, and Elsa was on her way to a career in photography.

WHO RECEIVED THE FIRST "OUTSTANDING WOMAN OF THE YEAR" AWARD?

Lynn Simons, Wyoming's Superintendent of Public Instruction, was named "Outstanding Woman of the Year" in 1983, by the Wyoming Commission on Women.

WHICH WOMAN IN 1986 HELD THE SECOND HIGHEST STATE OFFICE IN WYOMING?

Thyra Thomson, elected Wyoming's first Secretary of State in 1962, held the second highest office in Wyoming for more than twenty-four consecutive years.

Mrs. Thomson, whose husband was a U.S. senator-elect at the time of his death in 1960, was re-elected Secreatary of State in 1966. She received the "biggest majority ever received in Wyoming a candidate for a partisan office," according to the **Wyoming Blue Book,** Volume III (1974). The Secretary of State is the first in line of succession to the governor and is acting governor when the chief executive is absent from the state.

HAS THE WIND RIVER RESERVATION EVER HAD WOMEN FIRE FIGHTERS?

The 1974 Sho-Arap Fire Fighters' School at Fort Washakie trained its first women fire fighters. Of the 233 trainees, forty-two were women - forty Arapahoes and two Shoshones.

The jackalope has the long ears of a jack rabbit and the horns of an antelope, but is found in statue-form in a number of Wyoming towns, not on the prairie.

WHAT'S A JACKALOPE
and
OTHER WESTERN WORDS?

WHAT'S A JACKALOPE?

It's a furry animal that is shaped like a large jack rabbit with curved horns of a buck antelope. The trapper Ron Black was the first man to "see" a jackalope in Wyoming in 1851, so people say. When Black told his drinking cronies about the unusual creature, they shouted, "LIAR!"

There are jackalopes in this western state, but they don't hop like a jack rabbit or run like an antelope. They are statues, including one in the town of Douglas, where residents celebrate "Jackalope Day."

WHAT NAME IN THE WEST WAS
ONCE SYNONYMOUS WITH COFFEE?

Arbuckles. Many westerners considered it redundant to use the words, Arbuckles and coffee together. When describing the "ariosa" coffee, the owners of Arbuckle Bros. Coffee Company of New York City stated:

"The glazing, composed of eggs and sugar, not only retains the full strength and aroma of our coffee, but gives to it a richness of flavor unknown to other coffees; besides it saves the expense of eggs used in settling unglazed coffee."

WHAT'S A NESTER?

In the western part of the United States, a nester was a squatter, farmer or homesteader who settled in cattle-grazing country. During the late 1800s, cattlemen and nesters were in conflict. One of the most historic events in Wyoming's history pertains to the Johnson County War.

WHAT'S SISKEEDEE-AGIE?

The Crow Indian word for the glacier-fed Green River, in the southwestern section of Wyoming, means Prairie Hen River. There are at least four variations in the spelling of Siskeedee-Agie, including **Siskadee, Sheetskadee, Siskedo-azzeah** and **Seedskedee-agie.**

WHAT'S A CHINOOK?

A chinook is a warm, moist southwest wind which descends from the eastern slopes of the Rocky Mountains. Chinook is also the name of a North American Indian tribe living along the Columbia River.

Wyoming cattlemen, as well as other stockmen in the West, welcome a good chinook, especially if it comes from the north, melting the snow, thus allowing the cattle and sheep to reach grass.

WHAT'S A FALSE FRONT?

It's a wooden structure with a square front extending beyond the ridge of the roof of a building to give the effect of another story. Years ago in Wyoming, as well as in other states in the West, false fronted buildings were typical structures for stores on the main street. Both ghost towns, Atlantic City and South Pass City, in Fremont County, still have a few buildings with false fronts. Western movies with scenes of frontier towns often show streets with false-fronted saloons and stores.

WHAT'S A BOOTHILL?

Also known as a boot graveyard, boothill is a cemetery on the top of a hill near a frontier town in Wyoming, as well as in other camps and towns in the West. No doubt the word is associated with the man's wish to die with his boots on. Stephen Vincent Benet in "The Ballad of William Sycamore" wrote:

"I died in my boots like a pioneer,
With the whole wide sky above me,"

At one time in the American West, boots worn by the deceased often were nailed or tied to the wooden or stone cross over the deceased's grave. A few unmarked, as well as inscribed, graves of gold miners and their families are in boothill in South Pass City, now a ghost town.

WHAT'S A SAGE CHICKEN?

The correct name for this chicken-like bird of Western North America is sage grouse. It's also called sage hen and prairie hen. The large grayish grouse lives in open sagebrush country, and is identified by a black belly patch and spine-like tail feathers. Its flushing notes sound like **kuk kuk kuk**, but during the courtship display, male sage chickens make a popping sound.

The courtship of sage grouse, in late April and early May, in Wyoming is spectacular. While dancing, the male, much larger

This pine building with a false front is located on South Pass
City's main street. A gold mining camp once flourished here in
the early 1870s. The ghost town is now known as the South Pass
City State Historical Site.

than the female, puffs out his white chest and exposes the yellow air sacs on his neck, spreading his pointed tail feathers. Sage grouse is a favorite game bird, but the open season in late summer is for a very limited time.

WHAT'S A BUCK AND RAIL?

It's a pole fence supported by a sawbuck or sawhorse, having X-shaped legs projecting above the crossbar. The picturesque pine or cedar fences enclose many Wyoming ranches that often have more than a thousand acres. There are many buck and rail fences in the Teton National Park as well as in other areas of Western Wyoming.

WHAT ARE HOGBACKS?

They are long, narrow and somewhat steep hills. Another way to describe a hogback is that it is a ridge with a sharp summit and steeply sloping sides. There are hogbacks in many areas of this country besides Wyoming.

WHAT'S A SHEEP WAGON?

It's not a four-wheeled horse-drawn vehicle used to transport sheep! A sheep wagon is an enclosed canvas or metal-covered wagon on a wide wood base, with steel-rimmed wooden or rubber wheels. It is the sheepherder's home on the open range while he tends bands of sheep.

The interior of this one-room abode has a double bed, a built-in table that slides under the heavy wooden frame which holds the mattress in place. It also has low, box-like cupboards that double as benches, a small four-plate iron stove with an oven, as well as shelves nailed to the rounded stays over which the canvas or metal top is placed.

The herder generally lives in the covered sheep wagon year-round and most often his only companion is his faithful sheep dog, who guards the woolies from predators.

Not too many years ago, milions of sheep grazed in Wyoming's sagebrush and grassy plains. There were also many sheep wagons among them.

Some claim that now, in the late 1900s, more sheep wagons can be found in town and city museums than on the prairies and foothills.

Prized as an antique collector's item, the sheep wagon in many ways is the forerunner of the mobile home. The first sheep wagon was built in Rawlins, in Carbon County, probably about 1887.

Sheep wagons have been the setting for activities other than

The sheep wagon (featured on the cover) is an original pro-
duct of Wyoming, built in Rawlins about 1887, and is the forerunner of the modern mobile home.

herding. In the article, **"Wyoming's Old, Unique Weddings,"** from the pamphlet, **Buffalo Bones**, Kathy Martinez, on the staff of the Wyoming State Archives, Museums and Historical Department, wrote:

"The Sheep Queen of Wyoming, Miss Louisa Morrison, was united in holy matrimony on Jan. 19, 1901, with Ross Lambert. They were married in a sheep wagon near Casper at midnight."

Note: The author of this book, Lavinia Dobler, has a 1910 sheep wagon on her sagebrush-covered land, a short distance from her six-sided solid, log house in Riverton, with many windows facing the Wind River Mountains.

WHAT'S A "HAPPY JACK?"

Years ago early settlers in Wyoming and in other western states made their lamps or lanterns from tin syrup cans, using homemade candles for light. These useful lanterns were commonly called "Happy Jacks."

WHAT'S A RANCH?

It's an extensive farm, especially in the American West, on which large herds of cattle, sheep or horses are raised. A ranch is also any large farm on which a particular crop or kind of animal is grown.

One of the largest ranches in Wyoming is the Yellowstone Ranch in the eastern part of Fremont County. In 1987 the ranch had about one million acres of deeded and federal land that was leased along the Sweetwater River. Yellowstone Ranch sprawls over a 100-mile area, according to Fremont County records in the courthouse at Lander.

WYOMING'S
INDIAN LEGENDS

THE LEGEND OF "THE LAKE THAT ROARS"

Shoshone hunters were excited one early spring morning, countless moons ago, when they saw a huge white buffalo grazing among the dark brown bison near the glacier fed lake in the Wind River Mountains.

It was the first time they had ever had the chance to shoot a white bull, rare among the large, hoofed mammals with curved horns.

With moccasined feet the expert hunters, armed with bows and arrows, kicked their spotted ponies, and shouting wildly, raced toward the herd. They were determined to separate the white buffalo, with long shaggy hair on its broad shoulders, from the other bison.

The frightened bull lowered his massive head and dashed into the lake. In his attempt to get away from his pursuers, the white buffalo became exhausted, sank into the cold water and drowned.

During the below-zero weather, the wind whips the snow-covered blocks of ice on Bull Lake, lifting the frozen masses and dropping them; the noise sounds like a prolonged roar. Many Shoshone Indians' explanation is that the white buffalo's spirit is roaring with anger.

Bull Lake, on the Wind River Reservation in Fremont County, is often called "The Lake that Roars." *

THE LEGEND OF WIND RIVER CANYON

More than a hundred years ago, a young Shoshone chieftan and his sweetheart, whose long flowing hair was the color of obsidian, were walking along the winding river at the head of the many-colored Wind River Canyon in the Owl Creek Mountains. Suddenly the wind whisked an eagle feather from the girl's shining hair. Fascinated, the lovers watched the almost weightless object sail northward.

Later the wind dropped the feather on red earth beyond the rocky gorge, but the couple had no idea where the thunderbird's feather had gone.

When the lovers finally reached the area where they hoped to find the feather, to their great wonderment they watched a mist of cooling water vapor shoot out of the vermillion colored earth.

According to legend Indian hunters chased a huge white buffalo into Bull Lake, which is often called "The Lake that Roars."

Puzzled, they looked at each other in awe, believing that the Great Spirit had led them to the mineral spring. They bathed in the warm water and then hurried back to the Shoshone camp to tell their people about the healing qualities of the odd-smelling mineral spring.

The Shoshone families took down the many poles that supported their tepees made from buffalo hides, and set up a campsite near the spring.

Shoshone tribal members often boasted that their warriors and braves, who bathed in the mineral springs and others nearby, had greater physical strength and endurance than the Indian men from other tribes. Some people stilll claim that if a feather is released at the head of the chasm near Boysen Dam, it will float down toward the spring.

Wind River Canyon is one of the very few chasms in Wyoming with a legend. At one time Shoshone Indians hunted and camped in the wilderness by the glacier-fed river. A portion of the canyon is on the Wind River Indian Reservation, the home of the Shoshone and Arapaho Indians. *

THE LEGEND OF LAKE DE SMET

One summer day long ago, Little Moon, a handsome Indian brave of the Crow Tribe, and his true love, Star Dust, arranged to meet that afternoon at their favorite tryst by the edge of the mountain lake in the Big Horn Mountains.

The Crow maiden, with long, black, braided hair, was not only lovely in every way, but her brown eyes sparkled whenever she was with her beloved.

Later that day Little Moon sat by the lake, the blue-green water glimmering in the sunlight. While waiting for Star Dust, he saw the face of a young woman in the water. He not only was attracted to her, he thought she was the most beautiful Indian maiden he had ever seen. She smiled as though she were beckoning him to join her.

Just as Little Moon started to jump into the lake, his true love, Star Dust, touched his arm. Turning quickly around and scowling, he pushed her away, demanding that she return to their village. But when he turned back to face the sun shining on the water, eager to again admire the smiling face in the water, it had disappeared.

The next morning Star Dust's body was found on the edge of the lake. Heartbroken because his favorite daughter had drowned, legend has it that Star Dust's warrior father bound Little Moon to a huge boulder and left him to watch for the maiden the young brave thought he had seen in the water.

THE BEARS AT DEVIL'S TOWER

The Sioux people called the stone obelisk, formed by lava, **Mato Tipe**, meaning Bear Lodge. It is said that Sitting Bull, victorious chieftan in the battle of the Little Bighorn, "made medicine" at the tower, getting the gods' promise of victory in one of his most challenging campaigns.

In the Sioux version of Devil's Tower, three Indian maidens were gathering wild flowers when they saw bears ready to attack them. They ran to the huge boulder to escape from the dangerous animals. The gods, who realized that the Indian maidens were in great danger, caused the rock to rise high above the ground.

The bears tried to climb the boulder, but slowly the solid mass of stone rose higher and higher toward the sky. The bears, even with their strong claws, could not hang onto the rock. One by one they fell to the ground and were killed.

With the flowers the Indian girls gathered they braided a long rope and then slid down the tower. The Sioux people claim that the marks on the rock wall were made by the bears' strong claws.

THE MEDICINE WHEEL MYSTERY

If there were ever any legends about the medicine wheel, the mysterious, prehistoric shrine or altar probably was built "before the light came", to the people of long ago, "who had no iron."

Archeologists, who have studied the wheel-like formation, continue to be puzzled and mystified. They have no clues to tell them what ancient Indian tribe constructed the shrine or when it was formed. They believe however, that the primitive people probably were sun worshippers.

The Medicine Wheel, almost 250 feet in circumference, is located west of the city of Sheridan in the northern part of Wyoming, at the top of the Big Horn Mountains.

The three-foot-high central cairn of slate and stone probably represents the sun. Then from the center or hub, resembling spokes in a wheel, are 28 rocks which may be symbolic of the twenty-eight lunar days. There are six medicine tepees that circle the perimeter of the wheel that may symbolize the planets. The bleached buffalo skull faces toward the early morning sun. The buffalo has always had deep significance to the Plains Indians.

ARTS IN THE

FORTY-FOURTH STATE

WHO WERE WYOMING'S EARLIEST ARTISTS?

Indian artists used crude, primitive tools to draw or cut symbolic figures and animals on rocks and cliffs, as well as in caves and rock shelters. Pictographs and petroglyths are found in many areas of the state, including Castle Gardens, located about forty miles east of Riverton in Fremont county.

WHAT WERE WYOMING'S FIRST BOOKS?

The first books to be printed and published within the Wyoming wilderness were Indian vocabularies. The Army Press at Fort Laramie printed **The Dictionary of the Sioux Language** in 1864, a pamphlet with thirty-three pages.

Then in 1868, the Freeman Brothers, Leigh R. and Fred K., of Green River City, printed **A Vocabulary of the Snake, or Sho-Sho-Nay Dialect** by Joseph A. Gebrow, interpreter.

WHICH TETON PEAK IS NAMED
FOR A WESTERN LANDSCAPE ARTIST?

Thomas Moran, born in England in 1837, was seven years old when his family came to the United States. During later years Moran did some of his finest paintings in Wyoming. He accompanied F.V. Hayden's expedition to the Yellowstone region in 1871, the year before the scenic area was made a national park. From his sketches of his trip, Moran painted the large study, "The Grand Canyon of the Yellowstone," which was purchased by the U.S. Congress.

Because of Moran's contributions to the West, Mount Moran, the fourth tallest peak in the Grand Tetons, is named for him. In the early part of this century, a tourist village near the dam, located at Jackson Lake, the second largest lake in Wyoming, was called Moran. At Moran Junction in northwestern Wyoming, the highway to the north leads to Jackson Lake Lodge, Colter Bay and Yellowstone National Park. The highway to the south of Moran Junction leads to Grand Teton National Park and the mountainous town of Jackson.

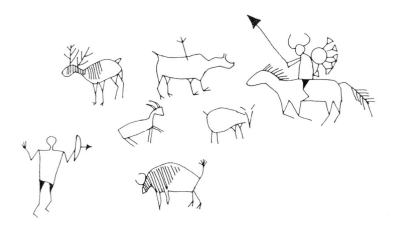

Figures like these were drawn long ago by people who hunted in wilderness Wyoming

WHAT TYPE OF 19TH CENTURY WYOMING BUILDING WAS TYPICAL OF THE REMINGTON ERA?

The sod-roof, chink-log construction was typical of one-story houses and barns on the ranches and towns in 1890, when Wyoming was admitted as a state. The structures were also the type of building popular when Frederick Remington was living in the West.

Remington worked as a cowboy, scout and sheepherder in the mountains and prairies. Born in Canton, New York in 1861, he was not only a painter, he was also a gifted sculptor, illustrator and writer.

Remington's subjects were drawn primarily from life on the Western plains, show horses, cowboys, Indians and soldiers in action. His paintings are exciting portrayals of the West and they have been extensively reproduced in prints.

Before Remington died in 1909, at the age of forty-eight, he had completed some 2,700 drawings. Replicas of his twenty-three bronzes are in many collections and museums in the United States, including the Buffalo Bill Historical Center in Cody.

Remington's studio in New Rochelle, New York, the gift of Lawrence Rockefeller, is on permanent display at the Buffalo Bill Historical Center. The Center is the finest museum in Wyoming, and ranks among the best in the nation.

WHERE IS THE NOVEL "WILD WIND, WILD WATER" SET IN WYOMING?

The town of Riverton on the Wind River in Fremont County is the setting for the first historical novel to be written about the 1906 government land lottery. The author, Lavinia Dobler, used the name Wind River instead of Riverton, because of the town's location near the river, the most important waterway in that section of Wyoming, east of the Wind River Mountains.

The book is written about the struggle the author's parents, George and Grace Sessions Dobler, encountered, along with other early Riverton homesteaders, who attempted to get water for their arid lands.

During the first land lottery in Wyoming, Dobler's number, "111", was drawn from a metal box on Saturday, August 4, 1906, on Main Street in Lander. He immediately filed on the claim of 160 acres and began proving up on his homestead, which was located in sight of Griffey Hill, a few miles west of town.

Wyoming Governor Fenimore Chatterton had envisioned a prosperous agricultural community in Riverton if canals were built. Banker and salt magnate of Chicago, Joy Morton, represented the Wyoming Central Irrigation Company, and the state engineer, Clarence Johnson, signed the contract on August 1, 1906, giving the company the right to build laterals on the sagebrush land north of the Wind River that had been formerly part of the Shoshone Reservation.

The campus of Central Wyoming College was the former homestead of pioneer lawyer and judge George F. Dobler. The town of Riverton was first called Wadsworth, for the Indian agent, but the name was changed to Riverton, the largest town in Fremont County.

Wild Wind, Wild Water was published by Bill and Jean Mead, Misty Mountain Press, Casper, Wyoming. The novel was among those selected to appear on the full-color Wyoming literary map of 1984, published by the University of Wyoming.

DOES WYOMING HAVE A STATE SONG?

Yes. The lyric, "Wyoming", was written by Charles E. Winter of Casper, with music by George E. Knapp, and adopted in 1955 as the state song by the thirty-third legislature, some sixty-five years after Wyoming became a state.

Winter, author of several historical novels about Wyoming, wrote the poem the summer of 1903, and Earle R. Clemens composed the music. The song was introduced during the summer at the State Industrial Association convention in Sheridan. The following year, 1904, the song was presented at the World's Fair in St. Louis.

Savilla King, paternal aunt of former president Gerald Ford, then a young girl whose home was in Casper, sang the state song on "Wyoming Day" at the Portland, Oregon, Fair, July 10, 1905. The daughter of the pioneer entrepreneur of central Wyoming, C.H. King, Savilla was dressed in a glamorous white Parisian evening gown with a long train.

In 1920, George E. Knapp, a professor of music at the University of Wyoming, wrote music in march tempo for Winter's poem and arranged it for group and chorus singing.

The first stanza: (from **Wyoming Blue Book**)

In the far and mighty West,
Where the crimson sun seeks rest,
There's a growing splendid state that lies above,
On the breast of this great land;
Where the massive Rockies stand,
There's Wyoming young and strong
The State I love!

Built in the 1890s, the Sheridan Inn is famous for its sixty-nine gables.

WHICH WYOMING INN DID RIPLEY CALL "THE HOUSE OF SIXTY-NINE GABLES"?

The Sheridan Inn, built during the 1890s, on the outskirts of Sheridan, was called "The House of Sixty-Nine Gables" by Robert Ripley. Located just south of the Big Horn Mountains, the Inn has many vertical triangles. In fact, the sixty-nine gable design makes the building unique as well as attractive.

The large wooden structure, with windows in the sixty-nine vertical triangles called gables, has a wide porch that runs along the front of the dark brown building and its south side.

Costing $75,000, Sheridan Inn was built by the Burlington and Missouri Railroad (now known as the Burlington Northern) and the Sheridan Land Company. Thomas R. Kimball, the architect from Omaha, designed the hotel to resemble an old country inn that he had admired while visiting Scotland.

When the striking and unusual Sheridan Inn opened, many claimed that it was one of the most interesting and finest hotels between Chicago and San Francisco.

Dressed in his elegant clothes, Colonel William Frederick Cody, better known as "Buffalo Bill" Cody, had the honor of leading the grand march for the first dance, Sunday evening, June 18, 1893. He owned Sheridan Inn between 1894-1896. For years the Inn was the center of social life, not only for the town of Sheridan, but for the surrounding areas.

Wealthy ranch owners, attired in black suits with tails, and women in colorful silk and satin evening gowns often danced the Virginia Reel and the Schottische (the round dance in three-quarter time).

Distinguished visitors who stayed at the Sheridan Inn were three presidents: Theodore Roosevelt, William Howard Taft and Herbert Hoover; Calamity Jane (whose real name was Martha Canary), Charles Russell, artist of the West; and Ernest Hemingway, famous author; as well as generals such as John J. Pershing, whose wife was Frances Warren of Cheyenne. She was the daughter of Francis E. Warren, the first elected state governor of Wyoming in 1890. At the time of his death in 1929, Senator Warren had served Wyoming in the upper house of Congress for thirty-seven years, the longest service record, at that time, in the U.S. Senate.

In 1964, Sheridan Inn was recognized as a National Landmark. However, the next year it was not operated as a hotel. Then, in 1967, Mrs. Neltje Kings purchased the fine historic building and it reopened officially in 1969. (Source: **Wyoming, A Guide to Historic Places**, Wyoming Recreation Commission).

WHOSE PHOTOGRAPHS CONVINCED CONGRESS TO SET ASIDE YELLOWSTONE?

Photographs taken by William H. Jackson during the 1870s while he was a member of the F.V. Hayden expedition, helped to convince Congressmen that Yellowstone should be set aside as a national park.

Born in Keeseville, New York, in 1843, Jackson is recognized as one of the best early photographers of the American West. As a young man he devoted his life to recording the scenic grandeur and historic sites of the West, and settled in Omaha, Nebraska in 1868.

Among many photographic studies, Jackson took pictures of the building of the Union Pacific Railroad across southern Wyoming. When photographing the peaks of the Tetons and other points in the northwestern part of the state, he and his men used horse-drawn wagons to carry cameras and other gear, but later switched to mules, one of whom was called Molly.

The artist took photographs of South Pass City when the gold mining camp was one of the largest in the territory. He climbed a rocky point, east of South Pass City, and took a photo of the wooden buildings that lined the main street. The photograph is considered one of the best ever taken in the early 1870s, during the boom period.

Impressed with his artistic ability, state officials commissioned Jackson in 1892, to take a series of photographs of Wyoming scenery to be exhibited in the 1893 Columbian Exposition in Chicago.

WHO WERE' "WYOMING'S MUSICAL AMBASSADORS" IN THE YEAR 1967?

The state legislature officially proclaimed the Casper Troopers as "Wyoming's Musical Ambassadors" in 1967.

The Troopers received the Veterans of Foreign Wars National Titles the year before, and they placed second in the World Open Championship. In 1965, the drum and bugle corps won the World Open and took many titles during their eastern state tour.

James E. Jones, founder and director, organized the Casper Troopers, a group of boys and girls ranging in age from 12 to 21. According to **The Wyoming Blue Book**, Volume III:

> "Jones, a building contractor, had the theory that the corps would be an excellent character-building activity for Casper young people. The dedicated Troopers work hard and practice rigid self discipline.

This had produced a unique 130-member marching unit that has captured world honors and has become a source of pride for all of Wyoming."

WHICH ACTOR WAS A CLOSE FRIEND OF MANY WYOMING NATIVE AMERICANS?

Cowboy actor Tim McCoy made his acting debut in 1922 with 500 Arapaho, Shoshone and Bannock Indians he recruited for the movie, "The Covered Wagon". The movie was the first of several filmed on the Wind River Reservation.

A respected member of the Arapaho tribe, Goes in Lodge, adopted McCoy as his blood brother. They remained close friends for many years. Two sons of Chief Washakie, Dick and Charlie, were also good friends of Tim McCoy and they acted in many films together.

Two Arapaho men, Tom Crispin and Mike Goggles, taught McCoy sign language, and the Goggles family, besides appearing in some Hollywood movies, were in demand at many events to display their Indian dancing. By erecting their tepee and performing, they assisted McCoy in the early establishment of the famous "Frontier Days" celebration, held annually during July in Cheyenne.

WHICH CELEBRATED SHAKESPEAREAN ACTOR PLAYED "HAMLET" IN CHEYENNE?

Edwin Booth played the title role in the Shakespearean production of "Hamlet" in 1887 at the Cheyenne Opera House. The playbills were printed in silk as well as on fine paper.

Frances E. Warren, wealthy cattleman, was serving as treasurer of Wyoming Territory in 1882 when he built the opera house.

Edwin Booth was the brother of the actor and Confederate sympathizer, John Wilkes Booth, who assassinated President Abraham Lincoln on Good Friday, April 14, 1865, at Ford's Theatre in Washington, D.C.

WHICH WYOMING JOURNALIST WAS KNOWN AS A BEST 19th CENTURY WIT?

Edgar Wilson Nye, better known as Bill Nye, was born in Maine, and lived in Wisconsin for twenty-four years before he mirgrated to Wyoming Territory in 1876.

Nye was admitted to the Wyoming bar and became a judge. He also edited the Laramie Boomerang for three years, a newspaper he founded and used to produce his humerous comments and yarns about frontier life.

Collections of his works appeared in **Bill Nye and Boomerang** (1881), **Forty Liars and Other Lies** (1882) and **Baled Hay** (1884).

The humorist moved to New York City in 1896 and wrote for the **World** newspaper. He also gave lyceum and recitals, some of them with poet James Whitcomb Riley.

WHO HAS A FINE COLLECTION OF INDIAN WEARING APPAREL IN WYOMING?

Jeri Greeves, a Kiowa and member of the Wyoming Arts Council, has an art gallery and trading company for Indian arts and crafts, with her huband Richard, at Fort Washakie, on the Wind River Reservation in Fremont County.

Over fifty costumes are now found in Jeri Greeves' twenty-year collection of Native American wearing apparel. Her first Kiowa dresses were acquired while working as a teenager at the Southern Plains Indian Museum at Anadarko, Oklahoma.

One striking costume Mrs. Greeves models is a South Arapaho ghost dance dress. Her great-grandmother wore the dress during the late 1800s when ghost dances were still practiced. The Pauite Messiah Wovoka of Nevada in 1889 introduced the ghost dance as a religious ceremony.

According to Jeri Greeves, the specifics of the ghost dance and ceremony have been lost because her great-grandmother died before she could pass on the knowledge to Jeri's mother, who was being groomed for the role.

Mrs. Greeves has purchased some of the unusual dresses from Indian people who have come from various parts of the country to attend pow-wows, held during the summer months on the Wind River Reservation.

WHOSE SCULPTURE WAS GIVEN TO THE QUEEN DURING THE U.S. BICENTENNIAL?

Harry Jackson's famous bronze called "The Two Champions" was this country's gift to Elizabeth, the reigning queen on England in 1976, during the U.S. bicentennial celebration. Jackson is recognized as a successful sculptor of the American West. Jackson's bronze of Sacajawea, the Indian guide-interpreter on the Lewis and Clark Expedition, is in the Buffalo Bill Historical Museum in Cody, as well as on the campus of the Central Wyoming College campus in Riverton.

Jackson has also done a striking bronze of John Wayne, the movie actor. A miniature of the bronze is in the Arts Center Building at Central Wyoming College.

Long before white men came into the wilderness now known as Wyoming, Indians were creating artistic drawings.

WHEN WAS THE
ST. STEPHENS INDIAN MISSION HERITAGE CENTER DEDICATED?

The Heritage Center was dedicated on May 20, 1984, highlighting the 100th birthday of St. Stephens Mission on the Wind River Indian Reservation, a few miles south of Riverton.

Arapaho collections include the old saddle used by Francis Setting Eagle, one of the early students at the mission in 1892. The collection of the **Wind River Rendezvous** magazines is also on display. The magazines are probably the single most popular source of information about the reservation and the life of the Shoshone and Arapaho people, according to the Reverend Anthony J. Short, S.J., director of the Heritage Center in 1984.

WHAT ARE SOME OF THE MOVIES WITH WYOMING AS THE SETTING?

A list of Wyoming films was compiled by Steven R. Peck, who for several years was movie editor of the **Riverton Ranger** special section, **Diversions.** Peck wrote, "Many movies with Wyoming as their settings have been made over the years." A few of the best-known include:

HEARTLAND (1970)

This film received rave notices at a number of film festivals, then won over a major studio which agreed to distribute it.

"Heartland" stars the accomplished character actor, Rip Torn, and Conchata Farrell. The film director was Richard Pearce.

HEAVEN'S GATE (1980)

This film is perhaps the most famous flop in film history. "Heaven's Gate" has come to symbolize filmmaking extravagance. A dramatized account of the famous Johnson County range war, the film was directed by Michael Cimino, an Oscar-winner for the film, "The Deer Hunter" in 1978.

The film, which almost single-handedly destroyed United Artists Studio, stars Kris Kristofferson, Cristopher Walken and Isabel Huppert.

BADLANDS (1973)

Director Terrence Malick adapted the true story of the Charles Starkweather murder case from the 1950s for the screen.

A madman, played by Martin Sheen, killed a number of innocent people and fled to the barren Wyoming badlands near Douglas, where he was apprehended.

WAR PAINT (1926)

This movie was filmed near Fort Washakie on the Wind River Reservation. Among the Native Americans who were in the film were Bad Teeth, Goes-in-Lodge, Night Horse and George Wallowing Bull, all members of the Arapaho tribe.

TOM HORN (1980)

Steve McQueen played Horn, the legendary prairie lawman who was revered by some, hated by others. Many scenes of the famous bounty hunter's life were shot in Wyoming, but the film's photography is its redeeming factor.

Directed by William Wiard, it was Steve McQueen's next-to-the-last film before he died.

THE MAN WHO LOVED CAT DANCING (1973)

Burt Reynolds, Sarah Miles, Lee J. Cobb, and George Hamilton starred in this enjoyable Western film concerning a defiant woman who takes up with a bunch of hard-nosed outlaws.

The film is based in Wyoming and features Jay Silverheels, who played Tonto on the popular "Lone Ranger" TV series. The film's director was Richard Sarafian.

RAGE (1972)

George C. Scott directed and starred in the modern-day tale about a Rawlins area rancher who is exposed to nerve gas, along with his young son. His rage comes when neither the government nor military authorities will help him. You'll recognize some of the scenery around Bairoil, Wyoming.

WYOMING (1940)

Here's another routine Western, which stars character actor, Wallace Beery, and his sidekick, Leo Carrillo. Richard Thorpe directed the story of on-again, off-again friends.

WYOMING (1947)

"Wild Bill" Elliot stars with Vera Ralston and Gabby Hayes in this pretty good Western drama that pairs off homesteaders and ranchers. Joseph Kane was the director.

WYOMING RENEGADES (1955)

This, unfortunately, is the worst of the films with Wyoming in the title. An ex-outlaw, played by Phil Carey, tries to go straight. Fred Sears was the director.

THE VIRGINIAN (1929)

The first of two versions of the Owen Wister novel was among the very first talking Westerns ever made. It stars a very young Gary Cooper, and is directed by Victor Fleming, who later directed "Gone With the Wind" and "The Wizard of Oz", among others.

THE VIRGINIAN (1946)

Joel McCrea stars in the remake of the 1929 film. This one's not quite so good or famous as the original.

THE SHERIFF OF FRACTURED JAW (1959)

One of the last films directed by the great Raoul Walsh, this Western spoof is based on the fictitious Wyoming Town of Fractured Jaw. An Englishman is given the unenviable job as sheriff and it makes for a few laughs. Kenneth More, Jayne Mansfield and Robert Morely are featured.

CHEYENNE (1947)

A gambler attempts to catch a crook for bounty, then ends up falling in love with the outlaw's wife. This standard Western, also directed by Raoul Walsh, stars Dennis Morgan, Jayne Wyman, Alan Hale and Arthur Kennedy.

CLOSE ENCOUNTERS OF THE THIRD KIND (1977)

This spectacular, imaginative sci-fi movie involves a group of alien visitors who land on Devil's Tower near the town of Moorcroft. Steven Spielberg directed this winner which stars Richard Dreyfuss.

CHEYENNE AUTUMN (1964)

The legendary John Ford, one of the finest directors in American film history, directed this Western during the twilight of his career.

Richard Widmark, Carroll Baker, Edward G. Robinson and Sal Mineo are featured, along with several famous cameo performers.

THE CHEYENNE SOCIAL CLUB (1970)

This Western comedy teamed James Stewart and Henry Fonda for the only time in their careers. The drifter (Stewart) is called to Cheyenne to take over his dead brother's business. This engaging comedy was directed by Gene Kelly.

ANY WHICH WAY YOU CAN (1980)

Clint Eastwood stars in this sequel to "Every Which Way But Loose". The comedy film ends up with the characters staging a spectacular fist-fight in downtown Jackson. Several well-known Wyoming citizens appear in this film.

THE MOUNTAIN MEN (1980)

This rather dismal historical piece about the mountain men of the Wind River Range stars Charleton Heston and Brian Keith as eccentric trappers who come into civilization just once a year.

Richard Lang directed this baddie, which is fraught with inaccurate details about the state and has some comical mispronounciations of familiar place names.

SHANE (1953)

Considered perhaps the finest classic Western ever made, "Shane" is based in spectacular Jackson Hole near the Teton Mountains. Alan Ladd stars as a gunfighter caught in a land where gunfighters are a dying breed.

Van Heflin, Jean Arthur and Brandon DeWilde are the family he protects, with Jack Palance playing one of the most deliciously evil bad guys in film history.

Famed director George Stevens was behind the camera for this one.

THE WILD COUNTRY (1971)

Based on the "Little Britches" book series, the Disney movie features Steve Forrest, Ronny Howard and Vera Miles as a family moving from Pittsburg to Wyoming. Much of this film was shot in Fremont County, and the name of the Dubois rancher, Ab Cross, was borrowed for a character in the film. Robert Totten directed.

HAVE ANY OTHER MOVIES BEEN FILMED IN THE TETON-JACKSON HOLE AREA?

An article, "Western Film Classics" in the magazine **Teton,** (Volume 16, 1984), lists a number of films, including the following:

BIG TRAIL (1940)

This was the first time John Wayne starred in a movie with the Jackson Hole country as the setting. Made in the 1940s, Marguerite Churchill plays John Wayne's sweetheart, experiencing pioneer hardships along the well-traveled Oregon Trail. Ward Bond and Tyrone Power had minor roles.

BAD BASCOMB (1946)

Wallace Berry stars in this action-packed movie, filmed near Moose on the Snake River. Lots of action in this film includes horses that stampede, bridges that collapse and brawls in rustic saloons as well as explosions in the countryside.

BIG SKY (1952)

Starring Kirk Douglas, this film tells the story of a boat expedition in the "Mandan" of more than a thousand miles along the Snake River and on Jackson Lake.

THE FAR HORIZONS (1955)

This movie, which relates to the 1803-1806 Lewis and Clark Expedition, stars Charleton Heston, Fred McMurray and Donna Reed, who play historic roles. It was filmed on the Snake River not far from Dead Man's Bar.

JUBAL (1956)

Glenn Ford, Rod Steiger, Ernest Borgnine and Noah Beery, Jr., are the stars. The setting was the Triangle X Guest Ranch, north of Moose.

SPENCER'S MOUNTAIN (1963)

In this movie, Henry Fonda and Maureen O'Hara are the parents of eight children, with James MacArthur, the oldest son (for whom Henry Fonda is desperately trying to raise money for college). The new minister in the town is Wally Cox.

AUTHOR'S NOTES

In deciding on the questions to be answered in my book, **Didn't Know That About Wyoming,** I selected some of the facts that make this state unique, interesting and very special.

The selection was a challenge. There are more than 150 questions with answers - from the time this area was an unexplored wilderness, later a territory, and finally in 1890, the forty-fourth state in the union, and into the Twentieth Century. I have also included several Indian legends.

My grateful thanks to Steve Peck, Associate Publisher of the **Riverton Ranger**, for writing the material about movies that pertain to Wyoming, and Jean Brainerd, researcher, Wyoming State Museums, Archives and Historical Department in Cheyenne, who helped to verify facts.

The books I used most extensively were **History of Wyoming**, by Dr. T.A. Larson, esteemed historian who has served in the Wyoming State Legislature; **Documents of Wyoming Heritage** by Charles Hall, Wyoming Bicentennial Commisson, 1976; **Wyoming: A Guide to its History, Highways and People**, Agnes Wright Spring and Dee Linford, editors, compiled by the Writers' Workshop Program of the Works Projects Administration in the State of Wyoming; **Wyoming Blue Book,** in three volumes, 1974, Wyoming State Archives and Historical Department; **Rocky Mountain Rendezvous: A History of the Fur Trade 1825-1840**, written by Fred R. Gowans, Brigham Young University Press, 1976.

Lavinia Dobler

April 17, 1987
at Winged Moccasins
Riverton, Wyoming

SOURCES

Allyn, Mary J., **Twentieth Century Pioneering, Our Frontier Days Experiences at Riverton, Wyoming,** (Riverton: 1956).

Beach, Cora M., **Women of Wyoming,** in two volumes, (Casper: S.E. Boyer & Co., 1927-1929).

Bonney, Orrin H. and Lorraine, **Guide to the Wyoming Mountains and Wilderness Areas** (Denver: a Sage book published by Alan Swallow, 1960).

Burgess, Florence F., Dobler, Lavinia, Vincent-Haas, Geraldine Williamson, Rosemary, editors, **Family Stories, Riverton, Wyoming, 1906-1981,** (Riverton: Riverton Senior Citizens Center, 1981).

Casper Star-Tribune, (Casper: 1984), selected newspaper articles.

Coutant, C.C., **History of Wyoming and the Far West,** (Laramie: Caplin, Spafford & Mathison, 1899).

Coutant, C.C., **Progressive Men of Wyoming** (Chicago: A.W. Bowen & Co., 1903). Coutant is believed to have prepared this large volume.

Craighead, John J. Craighead, Frank C. Jr., and Davis, Ray A., **A Field Guide to Rocky Mountain Wildflowers** (Boston: Houghton Miflin Co., 1963).

Dobler, Lavinia, **Wild Wind, Wild Water,** (Casper: Misty Mountain Press, 1983).

Drury, Clifford M., **First White Women Over the Rockies,** 3 volumes (Glendale: The Arthur H. Clark Co., 1963-1966).

Gowans, Fred R., **Rocky Mountain Rendezvous: A History of the Fur Trade Rendezvous 1825-1840,** (Provo, Utah: Brigham Young University Press, 1975).

Grant, Bruce, **The Cowboy Encyclopedia: The Old and New West from the Open Range to the Dude Ranch,** (Chicago: Rand McNally & Co., 1951).

Hall, Charles, **Documents of Wyoming Heritage,** (Cheyenne: Wyoming Bicentennial Commission, 1976).

Howard, Robert West, **The South Pass Story,** (New York: G.P. Putnam's Sons, 1968).

Jost, Loren, editor, **Exploring Fremont county History,** Vol. I and Vol. II, (Riverton: Central Wyoming College, 1982, 1983).

Jost, Loren, editor, **Exploring Fremont County History,** Vol. I and **ton, Wyoming,** as told by contemporary newspaper accounts during the years 1906-1953. (Riverton: compiled by members of the Riverton Historical Research Committee, 1981).

Larson, T.A., **History of Wyoming,** second edition, revised, (Lincoln: University of Nebraska Press, 1978).

Linford, Velma, **Wyoming: Frontier State,** (Denver: The Old West Publishing Co., 1947).

Mead, Jean, **Wyoming in Profile,** (Boulder: Pruett Publishing Co., 1982).

Mitchell, Finis, **Wind River Trails,** (Salt Lake City: Wasatch Publishing, Inc., 1975).

Murray, Larry, director of Curriculum Development Workshop, **The Wind River Reservation: Yesterday and Today.**

Peck, Robert, publisher, **(Riverton RAnger:** specific articles from the newspaper).

Pence, Mary Lou and Homsher, Lola M., **The Ghost Towns of Wyoming,** (New York: Hastings House, 1956).

Roberts, Phil, editor, **More Buffalo Bones,** (Cheyenne: Wyoming State Archives, Museums and Historical Department, 1982).

Short, Anthony, S.J., editor, **Wind River Rendezvous** (magazine), Vol. XIV, No. 2, April, May, June, 1984 (Riverton: St. Stephens Indian Mission Foundation, 1984).

Spring, Agnes Wright and Linford, Dee, **Wyoming: A Guide to its History, Highways and People** (New York: Oxford University Press, 1941). Compiled by the Writers' Program of the Work Projects Administration in the State of Wyoming).

Sniffen, William, publisher, **Wyoming State Journal,** (Lander: 1984), selected articles by Tom Bell printed in newspaper about Lander's 100th anniversary.

Thompson, Edith M. Schultz and Thompson, William Leigh, **Beaver Dick: The Honor and the Heartbreak**, (Laramie: Jelm Mountain Press, 1981).

Van Burgh, J.R., publications coordinator, **Sketches of Wyoming: A Collection of Pen and Ink Drawings,** accompanied by prose and poetry, (Casper: Field Science Foundation).

Trenholm, Virginia Cole, editor, **Wyoming Blue Book**, in three volumes. Reprint of Part I, Part II of **Wyoming Historical Blue Book**, by Marie Erwin, (Cheyenne: Wyoming State Archives and Historical Department, 1974). Volume I, **Acquisition of Land Through Territorial Days;** Volume II, **Statehood until 1943;** Volume III. **The Supplement** was compiled principally from data found in the State Archives and Historical Department.

Urbanek, May, **Ghost Trails of Wyoming,** (Boulder: Johnson Publishing Co., 1978).

Urbanek, Mae, **Wyoming Place Names,** (Boulder: Johnson Publishing Co., 1947).

Watts, Peter, **A Dictionary of the Old West, 1850-1900,** (New York: Alfred A. Knopf, 1977).

Western Writers of America, **The Women Who Made the West:** Stories of Unsung Heroines of the American West, (New York City: Doubleday & Co., Inc., 1980), introduction by Nellie Snyder Yost.

Wyoming Recreation Commission, **Wyoming Registry of Sites Enrolled in the National Register of Historic Sites,** (Cheyenne: Wyoming Recreation Commission, May 1984).

Wyoming Recreation Commission, **Wyoming: A Guide to Historic Sites,** (Basin: Big Horn Publishers, 1976). Introduction by Paul H. Westedt, Director, Wyoming Recreation Commission.

Wyoming Writers, Roberta Cheney and Emmie D. Mygatt, editors, **This is Wyoming, Listen . . .** contents contributed by members of Wyoming Writers, (Basin: Big Horn Books, 1977).

ABOUT THE AUTHOR

Lavinia Dobler is a Wyoming native and with her sister, Virginia, were the first twins born in the frontier town of Riverton in 1910. Her parents, George and Grace Sessions Dobler, were among pioneers in 1906 who each won 160-acre tracts of land in the government lottery, and proved up on their homesteads. George Dobler, a lawyer, later served as a judge and state legislator from Fremont County.

Lavinia was a news reporter, teacher, English supervisor in Puerto Rico, and research librarian for many years for Scholastic Magazines in New York City. Her juvenile novel, **A Business of Their Own**, won the 1957 Dodd-Mead "National Librarian of the Year" award and she was honored by Wyoming Writers with the "Emmie Mygatt" award in 1981. She received the "Medallion of Honor" award from Central Wyoming College in 1977.

Among her three dozen juvenile books, she authored a number of reference and textbooks, including: **When Greatness Called - Stories of Courage in America, National Holidays Around the World,** and the **Arrow Book of the United Nations,** a readable reference book about the world peace organization.

Customs and Holidays Around the World was listed by the Saturday Review of Literature as one of the best reference books of the year in 1964. It is still used extensively and can be found on the shelves of many libraries throughout the country.

The author's last book, **Wild Wind, Wild Water,** dramatizes the story of her parents' struggle, with other homesteaders, to bring irrigation water to the Riverton area north of the Wind River.

INDEX

Eleventh Ohio Cavalry, 39
Elliott, "Wild Bill, 91
Encampment Valley, 36
Ethete, Wy., 14, 30
Evans, Dr. John, 1
Evanston, Wy., 52

Farlow, "Stub", 32
Farrell, Conchata, 90
Ferguson, Miriam Wallace, 65
Fitzpatrick, Thomas, 54
Flathead Indians, 17
Fleming, Victor, 92
Fonda, Henry, 92, 94
Ford, Gerald, Sr.37
Ford, Glenn, 94
Ford, John, 92
Ford, Pres. Gerald, 37, 83
Forrest, Steve, 93
Fort Bonneville, 55
Fort Bridger, 23, 24
Fort Caspar, 26
Fort Caspar Museum, 26
Fort D.A. Russell, 25
Fort Fetterman, 25, 26
Fort Francis E. Warren, 25
Fort Hall, 17
Fort Kearney, Neb., 25
Fort Laramie, 4, 9, 22, 23, 24, 25, 45, 46, 81
Fort Manuel Lisa, 56
Fort Phil Kearney, 67
Fort Smith, 39
Fort Sutter, 55
Fort Washakie, 17, 30, 35, 44, 56, 66, 88, 91
Fort William, 9
Fossil Butte, 64
Fossil Butte Monument, 1
Freeman, Fred K., 81
Freeman, Leigh R., 81
Fremont, Capt. John C., 9, 21, 44, 50
Fremont County, 2, 6, 11, 14, 17, 25, 25, 32, 35, 37, 43, 44, 46, 47,
    48, 50, 58, 61, 65, 66, 71, 75, 77, 81, 82, 83, 88, 93
Fremont Peak, 50
Frison, George, 36

King, Leslie L., 37
King, Savilla, 83
Kings, Mrs Neltje, 85
Kinnear, Napoleon Bonaparte, 66
Kinnear, Wy., 25, 66
Kiowa Indians, 17, 88
Knapp, George E., 83
Kristofferson, Kris, 90

Ladd, Alan, 93
Lake DeSmet, 47, 48, 78
Lambert, Clement, 22
Lambert, Ross, 75
Lander, Frederick W., 46
Lander, Wy., 2, 36, 37, 44, 46, 50, 61, 65, 75, 82
Lander Cut Off, 24
Lander Valley, 61
Lanford, Nathaniel, 42
Lang, Richard, 93
LaRamie, Jacques, 45, 51
Laramie, Wy., 1, 41, 49, 59, 62
Laramie County, 33, 51
Laramie River, 45, 51
Larson, Dr. T.A., 23, 59
LeClaire, Iowa, 13
Lee, Edward M., 59
Leigh, Jenny, 42
Leigh, Richard "beaver dick", 42
Lejeuness, Basil, 22
Lemhi Pass, Idaho, 20
Lewis & Clark Expedition, 4, 19, 44, 56, 94
Lewis, Meriwether, 19
Lincoln, Pres. Abraham, 51, 87
Lincoln County, 5, 51, 63
Little Wind River, 44
Lowe, B.F., 46
Lucky McMine, 11
Lusk, Wy., 43

MacArthur, James, 60
Malick, Terrance, 90
Mammoth Hot Springs, 30
Mandan Indians, 56
Mansfield, Jayne, 92

NOTES

NOTES

NOTES

NOTES

For A Free Catalog of

WYOMING BOOKS

Write

210 South 4th St.
Box 48
Basin, Wy. 82410